P9-ELP-318

THE NEW POETIC
Yeats to Eliot

The New Poetic
Yeats to Eliot

C. K. STEAD

Professor of English,
University of Auckland, New Zealand

175/1740

upp

University of Pennsylvania Press
Philadelphia

PJC MILTON CAMPUS LRC

First published 1964 by Hutchinson & Co. (Publishers) Ltd.,
an imprint of Century Hutchinson Ltd.
Reprinted 1975, 1977, 1980, 1983.
Revised edition first published in the United States 1987
by the University of Pennsylvania Press,
by arrangement with Century Hutchinson Ltd.
© C. K. Stead 1964

Library of Congress Cataloging-in-Publication Data

Stead, C. K. (Christian Karlson), 1932-
The new poetic.

Bibliography: p.
Includes index.
1. English poetry—20th century—History and
criticism. 2. American poetry—20th century—History and
criticism. 3. Eliot, T. S. (Thomas Stearns), 1888-
1965—Criticism and interpretation. 4. Yeats, W. B.
(William Butler), 1865-1939—Criticism and interpretation.
I. Title.
PR610.S67 1987   821'.912'09   86-30865
ISBN 0-8122-1244-4

Printed in the United States of America

CONTENTS

FOREWORD
TO THE REVISED EDITION

The New Poetic, first published in 1964, was the product of, and a reaction against, a time when all literary studies, both in the universities and beyond, were dominated by the figure of T. S. Eliot. It would be difficult to exaggerate that dominance. In the journals of the 1950s you will find writers on almost any literary-historical subject referring to something Eliot had written, or said, or implied. Eliot had redrawn the map of English literature more radically than anyone had done since the Romantic movement. He had put the Romantics in their place—a relatively minor one. He frowned on Milton, smiled on Dryden. He had elevated Donne and the Metaphysicals. He had announced a new modern 'classicism', which his own poetry, it seemed, was supposed to exemplify, and which inherited the tradition of wit that went back to Jacobean times, while learning something as well from recent French Symbolism.

As a student in the 1950s I had been surprised, not by the picture itself, which clearly suited Eliot's own purposes as a poet, but by the completeness with which my teachers, like critics and scholars all around the English-speaking world, seemed to accept it. *The New Poetic* is an attempt to see modern poetry in general, and Eliot's poetry in particular, disengaged from the pressures of his own historical overview.

Although after the Second World War Eliot paid some sort of belated homage to Yeats, the other great English-language poet of the first half of the century, his critical programme had the effect of pushing Yeats off to the margins of the picture. And this view of Yeats as somehow marginal, or extraneous, had been confirmed by F. R. Leavis and the *Scrutiny* group. Since I was working in a Leavisite English Department (Bristol), I began *The New Poetic* with a chapter

7

asserting the greatness and centrality of Yeats as a figure in modern poetry. My method was, I suppose, to use a Leavisite argument against a Leavisite evaluation, and to show Yeats shunning the great public, and popular demands, in the interests of fidelity to complex and intractable truths.

Another effect of Eliot's criticism was to discredit the British Georgian poets, since they had been the rivals—the opposition camp—to his own and Ezra Pound's Modernism in the decade following the First World War. By the 1950s the word 'Georgian' had become exclusively a term of denigration. But my research showed that the early Georgians had themselves been innovators. They were in fact part of an honourable liberal-left tradition which included, for example, the novelist E. M. Forster, and War poets like Wilfred Owen, a tradition which passed on to W. H. Auden and the leftist poets of the 1930s.

But my main concern was Eliot himself. He had persuaded his critics that everything about his poetry was part of a conscious and deliberate 'classicism'; that apparent discontinuities were merely the omission of 'links in the chain'. Critics of *The Waste Land* had dutifully invented those links, explained what they believed it was all supposed to 'mean', and thus explained away the very qualities which made the poem distinct—its discontinuities and its mysteriousness. My own feeling for the poem told me that these readings were wrong, and that Eliot's famous Notes were more of a distraction than a help to anyone trying to deal with the poem critically. Further, as I read his criticism carefully, I found personal asides and fragments of literary autobiography confirming my own view of what kind of poem it was, a kind determined by the way its separate parts had been composed and the way they had been assembled. *The Waste Land* was the quintessential Modernist poem, which meant that its real antecedents were Symbolist and Romantic; whereas *Four Quartets* was a conscious attempt to structure another major Modernist poem, an attempt which (as I saw it) failed because, quite contrary to the popular notion of him, Eliot had no rationale, no theory, by which he could explain to himself what he had done in his earlier work. He had a rather severe and illiberal view of the history of English literature; and he had a strangely unpredictable way of arriving at something he could offer as a poem—and the two did not really suit one another. The critic and the poet were hardly the same man; and in his later years, I wanted to argue, it was the critic who took over the writing of the poetry.

These arguments were new and were not, of course, universally accepted when *The New Poetic* was first published. (The TLS reproached me for what it called my 'Jekyll and Hyde view of Eliot'.) But *The New Poetic* was bought and read and reprinted, and it has hardly been out of print in Britain since it first appeared. I think the rediscovery and publication of the manuscripts of *The Waste Land* has lent support to my view of the poem; and certainly in general the tendency has been away from the old Cleanth Brooks/George Williamson style of interpreting it. But the merit of *Four Quartets* is still a matter for critical debate. These are questions I have taken up again in a recent book, *Pound, Yeats, Eliot, and the Modernist Movement*. I am delighted that the University of Pennsylvania Press has decided to publish this new edition of *The New Poetic*.

C. K. STEAD
September 1986

As to the poetical Character . . . it is not itself—it has no self—it is everything and nothing—it has no character . . . A poet is the most unpoetical of anything in existence; because he has no Identity—he is continually informing and filling some other Body— the Sun, the Moon, the Sea and Men and Women who are creatures of impulse are poetical and have about them an unchangeable attribute—the poet has none; no identity . . . It is a wretched thing to confess; but it is a very truth that not one word I ever utter can be taken for granted as an opinion growing out of my identical nature—how can it, when I have no nature? . . .

. . . I will assay to reach the highest summit in Poetry as the nerve bestowed upon me will suffer. . . . All I hope is that I may not lose all interest in human affairs —that the solitary indifference I feel for applause even from the finest Spirits, will not blunt any acuteness of vision I may have. I do not think it will.

JOHN KEATS
*(from a Letter to
Richard Woodhouse,
October, 1818)*

Here, then, in this revolt against exteriority, against rhetoric, against a materialistic tradition; in this endeavour to disengage the ultimate essence, the soul, of whatever exists and can be realized by the consciousness; in this dutiful waiting upon every symbol, by which the soul of things may be made visible; literature, bowed down by so many burdens, may at last attain liberty, and its authentic speech.

ARTHUR SYMONS
*(The Symbolist Movement
in Literature, 1899)*

1

INTRODUCTION

'The rhetorician would deceive his neighbours,
The sentimentalist himself, while art
Is but a vision of reality.'

W. B. YEATS[1]

It is possible that a casual reader, taking up this book and reading here and there to discover its subject, might conclude that there was no subject, no developing and coherent statement on a single theme. Such a conclusion would be wrong, but understandable. In Chapter 2 the subject of my investigation is a single poet, W. B. Yeats. In Chapters 3 and 4 the focus shifts radically; the subject is not one man, but the condition of poetry in Britain during the years 1909 to 1916. In Chapter 5 the 'period' gradually narrows down to another single poet, T. S. Eliot, whose critical writings become the sole subject of Chapter 6, and whose poetry is studied in Chapter 7.

My justification for this apparently arbitrary shifting of focus is that the purpose of my research was to answer for myself certain questions. There was no way of knowing, until each section of the work had been undertaken, in what areas of study these answers would best be found. This book is a record of my research in those areas where answers presented themselves. The object of investigation changes, or appears to change, but the questions remain obdurately the same, and these questions, I hope, give the work its own peculiar coherence.

In this Introduction, then, it is necessary to indicate briefly the particular interests which prompted the research.

A poem may be said to exist in a triangle, the points of which are, first, the poet, second, his audience, and, third, that area of experience which we call variously 'Reality', 'Truth', or 'Nature'.

Between these points run lines of tension, and depending on the time, the place, the poet, and the audience, these lines will lengthen or shorten. At one time we may find the poet and his audience close together, and 'Reality' a great distance from them. This elongation of the triangle stifles the poem, and to a later age it will seem merely the product of an agreement between the poet and his audience to deceive themselves. At another time we will find the poet close to the point 'Reality', but the audience a great distance from them both. A later age is likely to declare of this poet that he was 'ahead of his time': but the distance of his audience will have caused some straining of the voice, as in the case of Blake. There are infinite variations, but (in so far as such a metaphor can be exact) the finest poems in any language are likely to be those which exist in an equilateral triangle, each point pulling equally in a moment of perfect tension.

The poets of this century have tended to see the great English public poets of the mid-nineteenth century as poets for whom (to apply my metaphor again) the triangle was seriously pulled out of shape. It has seemed to us that Tennyson and his audience, for example, were joined in a pact to deceive themselves about themselves and their society. 'Tennyson', T. S. Eliot says, 'is a very fair example of a poet almost wholly crusted with opinion, almost wholly merged into his environment'; his poetry suffers because he failed to approach his subjects 'with a mind unclouded by current opinion'.[2] In Tennyson's poetry Yeats can see only 'descriptions . . . of the moral law for the sake of the moral law', and an unwholesome 'brooding over scientific opinion'.[3] In this view of the great Victorian poets, the poets and critics of the present century have behind them the Pre-Raphaelite Brotherhood, and the Aesthetes of the 1890's.

In the last three decades of the nineteenth century the 'advanced' schools of English poetry strove so hard against the imbalance they believed the popular poetry of the time represented that a new imbalance was created, while the popular poetry continued unabated. Here the situation is complex. On the one hand the popular poets, their audience beside them, insist that the concern of poetry is 'Truth'; but their 'Truth', seen from this distance, seems most often an agreed middle-class simplification. On the other hand, the Aesthetes, concerned to remove themselves from the inhibiting demands of a conventional audience, insist that the concern of poetry is 'Beauty', a commodity, they imply, which only the Artist can truly perceive. By the 1890's Kipling and Wilde divide the world of poetry between them, and neither is complete. Kipling is, perhaps, the degenerate heir of that discursive impulse bred in the Romantic movement which encouraged the poet to be prophet and teacher to his people: 'degenerate' because he would teach nothing the people did not know, certainly nothing they did not want to know. Wilde, on the other hand, may be seen as heir to that other vocation of the Romantic poet: the call to discover, in moments of rare illumination, or Inspiration, a fragile image of Beauty. But again the heir is degenerate, for he insists that his image may not be brought into the world of men, and survive there. It is not surprising to find Yeats writing in June 1890 that 'the mind of man has two kinds of shepherds: the poets who rouse and trouble and the poets who hush and console'—and seeming content with neither.[4]

The Romantic movement, it seems, had split into two opposed impulses, and those impulses widened in their separation during the last years of the century. Their extremes lie immediately behind the poetry of this century, and, if my view of these matters is correct, one of the principal problems for twentieth-century poets has been to bring together those extremes, each of which, apart, constitutes a heresy. The branch had to re-knit. The pure aesthetic mode, like the pure rhetorical mode, was the product of a partial mind. In each the 'distances' were incorrect—the aesthete, far from an audience, subjected to the dictates of unorganized experience; the rhetorician, surrounded by the crowd, asserting hard abstractions which the sinuous complexity of experience failed to ratify. The best poets of this century have tried again to 'bring the whole soul of man into activity'. Unity has been the aim, fragmentation the enemy: hence, I believe, Yeats's concern with 'Unity of Being', and Eliot's with the undivided sensibility.

Together with this concern for wholeness of sensibility— hardly separable from it—there has been, in Yeats and in Eliot, a desire to re-establish a correct relationship between the poet and his audience. Where the audience stood too close, demanding flattery rather than truth, the poets have donned the hieratic robes of the aesthete, pushing their readers away from them, correcting the distance. Where the humanizing influence of a public has seemed remote and insubstantial, so that the poet's view of the world was in danger of becoming too special and literary, they have where possible beckoned readers towards them, relaxing the aesthetic posture, again adjusting the distance. Yeats, coming earlier than Eliot, had to live out the 'nineties, and reached his poetic maturity only at the age of fifty. But the progress of each has been, as we shall see, a gradual adjustment of an initial, necessary, aesthete's imbalance. The poet in each case has had to begin by finding a style—his own way of knowing and describing 'Reality'—and he has had to achieve this alone, since the common reader's idea of what a style should be simply would not serve. But once a style was achieved, an audience could be encouraged to understand it, though never to demand modification.

My concern in this study has been to look down the lines which run from the poet to his audience, and from the poet to his 'subject-matter', his world of experience. My first questions in each new area of study have been of this kind: What distance, what degree of independence, has the poet insisted on maintaining between himself and his audience? What circumstances have made this independence necessary? Has the distance been allowed to diminish as the poet gained in confidence? Have the best poets applied themselves to the task of pleasing a wide audience, to the edification of the few, or to pleasing themselves? My second set of questions is hardly divisible from the first, since the poet's attitude to his subject also involves, at the moment of composition, his attitude to his audience: From what area of experience ('Reality') has the poet drawn his subjects? How long, if at all, have these subjects remained narrowly personal, or in some other way esoteric, and at what point has he found it possible to write of 'popular' subjects—great public events, for example—or of contentious subjects like religion and politics? Where have such subjects been used without simplification into some popular framework of opinion or prejudice, and by what techniques of composition has such objectivity been achieved?

There is, of course, no simple set of answers to put against this simple set of questions. I have approached my subject with these questions in mind, not in the hope of reaching final conclusions but in order that my observations may fall into a coherent and meaningful pattern.

The poet is a man with a store of creative energy, which in

part he commits, and in part commits him, to a function which must be in one way or another a social function. My aim has been to define as nearly as possible what conception of the function of poetry is implied in the work of certain twentieth-century poets: and, in particular, to discern that function as it is implied in the work of Yeats and Eliot.

The general plan of what follows remains to be sketched. In the next chapter Yeats is studied as an isolated example of a great poet who faced and, in his own way, solved the problems indicated above. The aim of Chapters 3 and 4 is to observe the general literary situation during the years 1909 to 1916—important years, in the view this study has taken, during which new techniques of poetry, together with new critical ideas, helped to adjust the proportions of the literary 'triangle'. This general study is carried further in Chapter 5 in order that the literary context in which Eliot's most fruitful ideas were generated may be seen more clearly. Finally Chapters 6 and 7 attempt to arrive at a fresh view of Eliot's criticism and poetry, to see them not so much as a strange new 'classicism' blooming in the desert of post-war melancholy, but as another attempt to solve those fundamental problems, rooted in Romanticism, which have confronted all English-speaking poets of this century.

Chapters 3, 4, and 5—the general historical chapters—will, I hope, not only point forward, helping to explain what is to be observed in the study of Eliot, but will also cast a fuller explanation back over the preliminary study of Yeats. There is always something of a dialectic between the poet and his literary milieu, and without a feeling for this we can scarcely understand those critical positions he is forced to take up in relation to it.

Finally I shall try to draw out the single thread which I hope will be found to run without a break through this varied material, offering, in my final pages, whatever brief conclusions are not already apparent in the record itself.

REFERENCES

1. 'Ego Dominus Tuus', *Collected Poems*, Macmillan, 1952, p. 182.
2. *Selected Essays* (3rd enlarged edition, 1951), pp. 319–20.
3. *Ideas of Good and Evil*, 1903, p. 254.
4. *Letters to the New Island*, edited with an introduction by Horace Reynolds, 1934, p. 205.

2

W. B. YEATS, 1895–1916
An illustration of the problems

'. . . that violent energy, which is like a fire of straw, con-
sumes in a few minutes the nervous vitality, and is useless
in the arts. Our fire must burn slowly, and we must constantly turn away to think, constantly analyse what we
have done, be content even to have little life outside our
work, to show, perhaps, to other men, as little as the
watch-mender shows, his magnifying glass caught in his
screwed-up eye. Only then do we learn to conserve our
vitality, to keep our mind enough under control and to
make our technique sufficiently flexible for expression of
the emotions of life as they arise.'[1]

1. Poet and audience

'All day I'd looked in the face
What I had hoped 'twould be
To write for my own race'

IN YEATS's essay 'Certain Noble Plays of Japan',[2] written in
1916, two apparently contradictory sentences occur, five pages
apart:

'I love all the arts that can still remind me of their origins
among the common people.'

'Realism is created for the common people and was always
their peculiar delight, and it is the delight today of all whose

16

minds, educated alone by schoolmasters and newspapers, are without the memory of beauty and emotional subtlety.'

The sentences are interesting as an illustration of two attitudes Yeats held towards an audience for poetry. The contradiction results from carelessness rather than from any fundamental confusion of thought, and it disappears when we see that the 'common people' of the first sentence belong to Yeats's agrarian, feudal, folk ideal; while those of the second sentence are products of an urban, industrial society.

Yeats began his career as a poet with the aim of creating a literature that would be 'the possession of a people'.[3] He intended that his work should be widely read, that he should exist in the minds of the Irish as their national poet:

' . . . it would not have seemed worth while taking so much trouble to see my books lie on a few dining room tables . . . [Nature] filled my head with thoughts of making a whole literature . . . I wanted to write "popular poetry" . . . for I believed that all good literatures were popular . . . I hated what I called the coteries . . . I had a conviction, which indeed I have still, that one's verses should hold, as in a mirror, the colours of one's own climate and scenery . . .'[4]

This ideal remained with Yeats, and strongly asserted itself in the last years of his life. One sees it in the energy with which he went about producing his Cuala Press *Broadsides*, and in the pleasure he shows in his letters at being told (in 1937) that one of his Roger Casement poems was 'a ballad the people much needed'.[5] It is true that the ideal was modified by what he learned from the poets of the 1890's, so that in 1935 he could look back, with a typical mixing of irony and approval, on the poets who had restrained his earliest conception of what poetry should be:

'Poets said to one another over their black coffee—a recently imported fashion—"We must purify poetry of all that is not poetry" . . . Poetry was a tradition like religion, and liable to corruption.'[6]

The elderly poet, however, seems to have felt that he had himself become a 'popular' poet, that he had in fact achieved his earliest ambition. A new poetry had begun to appear in the 1920's which seemed to him so profound and difficult, and so determined to ignore public pressures, that by contrast with it he felt his own poetry had a wide and easy appeal. He had left the aesthetic tower of the 'nineties many years behind, and the new poetry of the 1920's and 1930's coming at a time when Yeats was trying to simplify his work, was for him only another kind of withdrawal. While Eliot was assuming a role that must have seemed to Yeats that of the 'poet's poet', Yeats himself was trying to return to something like the folk tradition. In his last years he would have agreed with the view he had expressed in an essay written in 1892, in which he rejected as 'not a literature of energy and youth' the art and poetry of England which, under French influence, were 'becoming every day more ends in themselves'.[7]

Yeats held consistently to the idea of a national literature, but, as Jeffares points out, at the same time (1892) that he was calling for a 'de-Anglicizing of our people' his poetic style was 'becoming more complex, and in an un-Irish direction'.[8] By 1895 he considered himself one of the Aesthetic movement he had earlier rejected. For the poets of this movement poetry was a private ritual, a way of life, rather than a social or national phenomenon. No considerations of the possible response of an audience were to influence the poetry. Yet, even in accepting his role as one of the aesthetic priesthood, Yeats retains elements of his earlier ideals. Contrary to dogma, he hopes to attract an audience into the temple. The following seems orthodox enough:

'We who care deeply about the arts find ourselves the priesthood of an almost forgotten faith . . .'

but it is immediately followed by

'and we must, I think, *if we would win the people* . . .'[9]

Writing in 1901, Yeats put forward the combination of these two ideals, the popular and the esoteric, which he held to for many years. Poetry commonly referred to as 'popular', he says, 'never came from the people at all'; it earned the epithet only by being widely read among the middle class. Longfellow, Campbell, Mrs. Hemans, Macaulay of the lays, Scott, and Burns are his examples—middle-class poets 'who have unlearned the unwritten tradition which binds the unlettered . . . to the beginning of time . . . and who have not learned the written tradition which has been established upon the unwritten'.[10] The true 'popular' literature (the folk tradition) is thus seen as something esoteric, unavailable to the 'common people' of the second of the two quotations above (p. 16).

In casting out all consideration of the large middle-class audience waiting to be pleased and instructed by its poets, Yeats is joining the 'nineties reaction against 'impure' Victorian poetry, with its 'descriptions of nature for the sake of nature, of the moral law for the sake of the moral law' and its 'brooding over scientific opinion'.[11] But he adds a further point which leaves room for a national poetry. The impurities of Victorian poetry, he suggests, are to be countered by a return to the source of poetry in the unwritten tradition; and this justifies his own looking to Ireland for the stimulus to write.

'There is only one kind of good poetry, for the poetry of the coteries, which presupposes the written tradition, does not differ in kind from the true poetry of the people, which presupposes the unwritten tradition.'[12]

By this manœuvre Yeats manages to hold his two allegiances; the Irish literary movement and the aesthetes are shut in one sentence, with their respective enemies, the Irish political balladists and the English middle class, left firmly outside.

Yeats is at this stage quite as uncompromising as his fellow poets in rejecting all thought of pleasing a general audience:

'Why should we thrust our works, which we have written with imaginative sincerity and filled with spiritual desire, before those quite excellent people who think that Rossetti's women are "guys", that Rodin's women are "ugly", and that Ibsen is "immoral", and who only want to be left in peace to enjoy the works so many clever men have made especially to suit them?'[13]

There is a mixture of truth and simplification in his attitude. The cities, he says, have taught people 'to live upon the surface of life'; the schools and newspapers have taught them to parrot opinions not their own. For the convenience of the argument only the middle class are now regarded as having political opinions, scientific interests, and newspaper vocabularies. The aristocracy and the peasantry, who retain contact with folk traditions, are without these 'impurities'. Again with Ireland in mind, Yeats is adding something extra to the doctrines of the 'nineties.

The attitudes expressed in these early essays are perhaps less interesting in themselves than they are as symptoms of an underlying desire for a relationship between poet and audience which would give the poet a recognized position within a community, but a position of independence. Yeats imparts a genuine sense of fragmentation when he writes about the English urban world; and if his representation of Irish society has less fact in it than dream at this point, the ideal it embodies is a reasonable one. Despite his continuing respect for the poets of the 'nineties, poetry for him is a social, and great poetry a national, phenomenon: 'Does not the greatest poetry always require a people to listen to it?'[14] And again: 'The poet must always prefer the community where the perfected minds express the people'.[15] But while seeking to write for, and from within, a particular society, the poet must not yield to pressure, put on him by that society, which would alter his individual insight. 'He must picture saint or hero, or hillside as he sees them, not as he is expected to see them.'[16]

Thus while Yeats continues to hope for a national literature and a national audience, his fundamental agreement with the judgement of the 'nineties on popular Victorian poetry does not allow him to hope for a *wide* audience:

'I had constantly tested my own ambition with Keats's praise of him who left "great verse unto a little clan" . . . we had nothing to do with the great public.'[17]

And he can even find justification for an esoteric poetry in the nature of the Irish genius:

'Ireland . . . could never create a democratic poet of the type of Burns, although it had tried to do so more than once . . . its genius would in the long run be distinguished and lonely.'[18]

During the years 1900 to 1910 Yeats's work for the Abbey Theatre broadened his conception of what this national literature should be, and made him more aware than he had been previously of the kind of people who were likely to form its audience. He continued to develop his 'dream of the noble and the beggarman', asserting in an essay written in 1907 that three types of men had created all beautiful things: aristocrats (beautiful manners), countrymen (beautiful stories), and artists ('all the rest').[19] These three groups alone were free from the materialistic, utilitarian attitudes that were destructive to literature. But at the same time he began more realistically to consider an audience outside these groups:

'My work in Ireland has continually set this thought before me: "How can I make my work mean something to vigorous and simple men whose attention is not given to art but to a shop, or teaching in a National School, or dispensing medicine?" I had not wanted to "elevate them" or "educate them", as these words are understood, but to make them understand my vision, and I had not wanted a large audience, certainly not what is called a national audience, but enough people for what is accidental and temporary to lose itself in the lump . . . Here there is the right audience could one but get its ears.'[20]

At this time Yeats was fighting in his own mind a battle against two extremes—'Burns's beerhouse' and 'Shelley's Chapel of the Morning Star'. He preferred the latter, but neither satisfied his desire for a poetry of wider and deeper appeal. He had always advanced the arguments of the 'nineties to resist pressure from the Irish patriots (Maud Gonne among them) who were often puzzled by his refusal to use poetry as a political weapon. But on the opposite flank he now countered extreme aestheticism with a more mature and vigorous concept of poetry:

'In literature, partly from the lack of that spoken word which knits us to the normal man, we have lost in personality, in our delight in the whole man—blood, imagination, intellect running together—but have found a new delight, in essences, in states of mind, in pure imagination . . .'[21]

The problem now presents itself to him as 'the choice of choices—the way of the bird until common eyes have lost us, or to the market carts'. It had not occurred to him so forcibly as a choice before, and it is partly out of this new tension that the stronger poetry of *Responsibilities* (1914) is written.

A clear realization of this choice comes to Yeats in imagining the response of countrymen (who had provided him and Lady Gregory with stories for their plays) to different kinds of poetry. They would, he says, have found more to please them in the stories of Homer than in Burns's ballads; and Villon could have delighted them with plays and songs, while Shelley's poems could only leave them puzzled. With this thought in mind Yeats states a new, more positive, compromise:

'We should ascend out of common interests, the thoughts of the newspapers, of the market-place, of men of science, *but only so far as we can carry the normal, passionate, reasoning self, the personality as a whole.*'[22]

He can now speak frankly of the 'nineties attitude as 'a misunderstanding'; and of the aesthetic doctrine in general as 'a good switch while the roads were beset with geese'.[23] The new willingness to acknowledge the presence of a wider audience is only a part of the total complex change Yeats underwent during these years. There is no doubt that his work for the Irish theatre helped to bring it about, and especially the association with Synge. Yet the performance of Synge's *Playboy of the Western World* made clearer than ever the difficulties of holding a national audience when the writer was not always prepared to flatter its opinions and echo its prejudices. The fierce stupidity of patriotic response made the determination to keep partisan arguments out of literature seem often hopeless. And the worst danger to poets still seemed to Yeats 'the approval of their fellows, which comes to them in full abundance only when they delight in general thoughts that hold together a cultivated middle class'.

The problem receives its fullest realization in the fine poem

'The Fisherman'.[a] The years of striving towards a national literature crystallize in the lines

> 'All day I'd looked in the face
> What I had hoped 'twould be
> To write for my own race.'

But against this is set an image of the 'reality'—the Irish audience as it is in fact, brawling, demanding, insensitive—

> 'The witty man and his joke
> Aimed at the commonest ear,
> The clever man who cries
> The catch cries of the clown,
> The beating down of the wise
> And great Art beaten down.'

In disgust with this scene Yeats calls to mind the fisherman who is both the man of action and part of that ideal community Yeats had thought might be created in Ireland:

> 'Maybe a twelvemonth since
> Suddenly I began,
> In scorn of that audience,
> Imagining a man,
> And his sun-freckled face,
> And grey Connemara cloth,
> Climbing to a place
> Where stone is dark under froth,
> And the down-turn of his wrist
> When the flies drop in the stream . . .'

The ideal is no longer sentimental, a refusal to face the fact that there is no such community, for the fisherman is

a *The Wild Swans at Coole* (1919): *Collected Poems*, p. 166. Critics of this poem have made the natural mistake of reading the line 'and the reality' to mean 'and *for* the reality'. In fact (as a letter to *The Times Literary Supplement*, 6 June 1958, points out) Yeats is contrasting the hope with the reality. 'Reality' points forward to the description that follows it.

> 'A man who does not exist,
> A man who is but a dream.'

Yet the poet's aim is still to write a poem for such a man, and for such a community:

> 'And cried, "Before I am old
> I shall have written him one
> Poem maybe as cold
> And passionate as the dawn".'

There is in this poem a tragic quality which springs from a full realization by Yeats of his position as a poet in the twentieth century. He has spent more than half a lifetime in the attempt to write poetry that might stand with the finest poetry of the past. Yet if it is to be achieved (and so far the finest still eludes him) it must be written for a man, for a community, that 'does not exist'.

'Nothing is more difficult and unwelcome', Shelley wrote in a letter, 'than to write without confidence of finding readers.' Yeats was never without this confidence, but his mind was frequently occupied with the *kind* of readers he was to find. Enriching the aesthetic doctrine of the 1890's to a point where it became something other than itself, and yet unable to return to his boyhood ideal of a poetry both national and widely popular, Yeats seems to have held an attitude to his readers which worked differently at different levels. There is the personal level seen in the frequently repeated statement (both in letters and in the prefaces to later plays) that the poet writes for 'a few friends':

> 'One writes and works for one's friends, and those who read, or at any rate those who listen [i.e. at the Abbey Theatre] are people about whom one cares nothing.'[24]

On this level the audience seems sometimes to be reduced in his mind to one person: 'If she [Maud Gonne] understood, I should lack a reason for writing . . .'[25]

There is also at times an element of aesthetic snobbery of the kind which prompted him in 1910 to write of 'One's own world of painters, of poets, of good talkers, of ladies who delight in Ricard's portraits or Debussy's music, all those whose senses feel instantly every change in our mother the moon . . .'[26] There is no doubt that Yeats felt himself shut out from the world where the results of one's actions could be seen in the form of positive changes, the world of politics, soldiering, even business:

> 'I turn away and shut the door, and on the stair
> Wonder how many times I could have proved my worth
> In something that all others understand or share;'[27]

He had chosen to be left out of this world, which be believed would impose its opinions on him and corrupt his poetry. But his rejection of it is more vehement because he knows how well his own abilities might have been used within it; and in compensation for his own sacrifice, he sometimes glamorizes the inner circle of the artistic life, the audience of the chosen few:

> 'How one loves Balzac's audience—great ladies, diplomatists, everybody who goes to grand opera, and ourselves.'[28]

The world in which Yeats moved personally, the inner community whose reactions he could feel at first hand, had to be a special one:

> 'If when my play is perfectly performed . . . Balfour and Sargent and Ricketts and Sturge Moore and John and the Prime Minister and a few pretty ladies will come to it, I shall have success that would have pleased Sophocles. No press, no photographs in the papers, no crowd. I shall be as lucky as a Japanese poet at the court of the Shogun.'[29]

This is the poet's milieu, not his wider audience; and it seems particularly for this group that Yeats wrote his later Noh plays:

> 'Fate has been against me. I meant these Noh plays never to be played in a theatre, and now one has been done without my leave . . . I had thought to escape the press, and people digesting their dinners, and write for a few friends.'[30]

But this narrower attitude could only be held because behind it
there is confidence that his work will be read by a wide audience,
scattered throughout the world, and that in the eyes of this
audience he has an identity as poet of the Irish literary renais-
sance.

There is a different attitude towards his Irish audience. The
response to Synge's *Playboy* is the most obvious of a number of
incidents which caused Yeats's frequent outbursts against 'The
daily spite of this unmannerly town', Dublin. He could never
rely on his Irish public to judge literature on literary standards,
and for twenty years he never sent his books to be reviewed by
Irish newspapers.[31] 'The Irish people were not educated enough',
he says, 'to accept images more profound, more true to human
nature, than the schoolboy thoughts of Young Ireland'.[32]

Yeats's position grows more and more clearly that of an Irish
poet who speaks to the world on Ireland's behalf. Throughout
his career Ireland is the object of his immediate attention. But he
achieves this almost in spite of Ireland, certainly in spite of many
of his Irish readers. Because of the peculiar difficulties of his
position, his purely literary development may be as well traced
against the background of London as against that of Dublin. The
changes in the London literary scene traced in Chapters 3 and 4
are, therefore, relevant to Yeats's own growth as a poet, and to
the growth of his attitude to his audience.

2. *Poetry and the public world*

> 'Nor may I less be counted one
> With Davis, Mangan, Ferguson,
> Because to him who ponders well
> My rhymes more than their rhyming tell
> Of things discovered in the deep'[33]

The brief summary above of Yeats's developing attitude to his
audience illustrates a problem for the twentieth-century poet.
To put the matter at its simplest, Yeats wants an audience, but
more than this he wants to write good poems; and the nineteenth-
century conventions of poetry had been such that good new

poetry was bound to disappoint the expectations of the reading public.

The history of Yeats's gradual acknowledgement of an audience is also the history of his development of a style which could handle themes of wider importance than those of a personal and private dream world. In his early years he resisted strongly any emergence of his art into the public world: first, because he was sure that a poetry (like that of the Irish political balladists) fully committed to a public cause, could never achieve the wholeness of Art; and second, because he feared that the poet who brought his work into close association with events in the public world would find public causes forced upon him. For Yeats, 'opinion', 'rhetoric', 'discourse', 'anecdote', were antitheses of poetry; they were of the will, subject to time and circumstance, while poetry was eternal. Yet the nineteenth century had trained its reading public to expect of poets all that Yeats most disliked:

'Longfellow has his popularity . . . because he tells his story or idea so that one needs nothing but his verses to understand it. No words of his borrow their beauty from those that used them before, and one can get all there is in story and idea without seeing them . . .'[34]

A period of withdrawal into himself was thus inevitable. Only with a style formed, and with confidence in his own direction, could a poet emerge into the light and pursue his own path undeflected.

Yeats's early hope for a wide audience came at a time when a lull in Irish political activity allowed him, together with Katherine Tynan and George Russell to start a literary movement which was 'national' but not 'political'. The hope died soon afterwards when the movement was attacked in Ireland for its policy of political non-commitment, and this coincided with the growing influence of the Aesthetes on Yeats. He withdrew into the Rhymers Club 'insistence upon emotion that had no relation to any public interest',[35] pointing out that scientific and political thought had brought with them in the nineteenth century 'a literature which was always tending to lose itself in externalities of all kinds, in opinion, in declamation, in picturesque writing . . .'[36] In reaction against this, he joined the search for 'certain qualities of beauty, certain forms of sensuous loveliness, separated from all the general purposes of life'.[37]

The attacks on him continued. In one of his letters he speaks of 'my special enemies, the Tower and wolf-dog, harp and shamrock, verdigris-green sectaries who wrecked my movement for a time'.[38] In defence he could only assert that the creation of fine literature was 'a greater service to our country than writing that compromises either in the seeming service of a cause'.[39]

Recalling his literary movement, and the attacks made on it by his countrymen, Yeats wrote some years later:

'The school of writers I belonged to tried . . . to begin a more imaginative tradition of Irish literature, by a criticism at once remorseless and enthusiastic. . . . Our attacks, mine especially, on verse which owed its position to its moral and political worth, roused a resentment which even I find it hard to imagine today, and our verse was attacked in return, and not for anything peculiar to ourselves, but for all that it had in common with the accepted poetry of the world, and most of all for its lack of rhetoric, its refusal to preach a doctrine or to consider the seeming necessities of a cause.'[40]

Critics have found it easy to dismiss the poetry of this 'more imaginative tradition', to see lines like

> 'Come away, O human child
> To the waters and the wild
> With a faery, hand in hand,
> For the world's more full of weeping
>   than you can understand.'

as the replacement of one unreal Ireland, that of 'shamrock and verdigris-green sectaries', by another equally unreal. But to see this early poetry as the product of mistaken ideas which held up the development of his best work is, I think, an error. In the light of his full achievement we must give Yeats the benefit of his genius, and acknowledge the correctness of his instincts. His later poems develop out of the faery poetry; and it was only the patient immersion of his mind in ancient traditions of poetry and mysticism that enabled him later to write with passionate, cold objectivity of contentious contemporary events which left his fellow poets, English as well as Irish, bewildered. Yeats, in these early years, divested his style of all he considered 'impure' in Victorian poetry; and since '*le style, c'est l'homme*', the process had to be a liberation of himself, a freeing of his mind from the common judgements and opinions of the world about him:

'I have always sought to bring my mind close to the mind of Indian and Japanese poets, old women in Connacht, mediums in Soho, lay brothers whom I imagine dreaming in some medieval monastery the dreams of their village, learned authors who refer all to antiquity; to immerse it in the general mind where that mind is scarce separable from what we have begun to call "the subconscious"; to liberate it from all that comes from councils and committees, from the world as it is seen from universities and populous towns . . .'[41]

It was by this process that Yeats was enabled (as Eliot has said of Blake) 'to approach everything with a mind unclouded by current opinion'.[42] For this reason, neither the relative weakness of many of his early poems, nor his own discontent with them in later life, can justify the view of his 'aesthetic' period as an absurd waste of time and talent. Yeats's progress towards the goal of great poetry was perhaps the most patient, tenacious, and logical of any poet in our literature. In Chapter 4 we shall observe a similar instinct among successive groups of poets—Georgians, and more radical Imagists—to narrow down the compass of poetry, to loosen its moorings in the public world, in order to purify it of abstraction and rhetoric. The pruning of all dead branches leaves the tree insignificant for a time, but makes way for fast new growth.

By 1910 Yeats had schooled himself sufficiently to be safe from what he considered the stylistic vices of his predecessors. He was ready to broaden the scope of his poetry, and this readiness made him impatient with his achievement. He began to feel discontented with the world-weariness, the undynamic voice characteristic of most of the poetry he had written. He compared his own poetic personality unfavourably with the personalities of seventeenth-century poets—'brisk and active men':

'Crashaw could hymn St Teresa in the most impersonal of ecstasies and seem no sedentary man out of reach of common sympathy, no disembodied mind . . .'[43]

For the emergence of his poetry from its narrow confines, Yeats gives credit to Synge. 'I did not see', he records, 'until Synge began to write that we must renounce the deliberate creation of a kind of Holy City of the Imagination.'[44] If Synge had not precipitated the change in Yeats, some other catalyst would no doubt have presented itself. But Synge's work excited Yeats: it had precisely the worldly vigour he envied in seventeenth-century poets, and none of the Victorian world-bettering and problem-solving.

'[Synge] was the man that we needed because he was the only man I have ever known incapable of political thought or of a humanitarian purpose.'[45]

Further, Synge was a writer of plays, and it was by a theory of dramatic intensity—the conscious adoption of a poetic persona, or 'mask'—that Yeats's poetry acquired a positive speech which was not the rhetoric of 'opinion':

> 'Pardon, old fathers, if you still remain
> Somewhere in earshot of the story's end . . .
>
> Pardon that for a barren passion's sake,
> Although I have come close on forty-nine,
> I have no child, I have nothing but a book,
> Nothing but this to prove your blood and mine.'[46]

Mr Frank Kermode, in his admirable book *Romantic Image*, has placed Yeats in a 'central Romantic tradition' which runs through the poetry of nineteenth-century France and reaches Yeats, Pound, and Eliot largely through the medium of Arthur Symons. The poets of this tradition have much in common with the earlier Romantics, but differ from them in 'abstaining from any attempt to alter the social order' and in despising what Baudelaire called 'puerile Utopias'.[47] Their poems stand 'free of intention on the one hand, and affective considerations on the other'.[48] The aim of these poets, often repeated during the 1890's, was to 'wring the neck of rhetoric'; 'opinion', 'abstraction', and 'rhetoric' go together in their critical writings, invariably with disapproval. These poets, Mr Kermode says,

'are in no position to teach, and indeed have a great dread of the didactic; but they have redefined the relationship of *utile* to *dulce*, and usually believe in their moral function, so that, in short, the pleasure communicated conduces to morality. That is why George Eliot, in some ways a typical Romantic artist, could call herself an "aesthetic teacher" and yet protest that she had no desire to instruct or change the world.'[49]

Mr Kermode is, of course, correct in placing Yeats in this tradition. The most constantly repeated idea in his prose writings is the necessity of allowing the poet freedom from single intellectualized positions, so that the imagination may be free to grasp the full complexity of life:

'We make out of our quarrel with others, rhetoric; but of our quarrel with ourselves, poetry.'[50]

And the Yeatsian 'mask' is in part a means of avoiding 'passive acceptance of a code'.[51]

Mr Kermode's principal task was to trace the particular tradition, and Yeats's place in it. Beyond this, a good deal remains to be said. Many kinds of writing range themselves within such a tradition: the difference between Yeats's early and late poetry is an example of the diversity of styles within a single mode.

The point I am concerned to make is one which Mr Kermode would, I am sure, understand perfectly, though it was not his concern to make it. Symbolist attitudes are central to Yeats's work; but Yeats is more than the sum of his antecedents. His poetry enters the public world as the work of no other Symbolist poet does. The conquest is unobtrusive, but complete. By 1916 Yeats's poetry had a hold on the public world which made his English contemporaries (Kipling, Austen, Watson, Newbolt, Noyes—poets who despised 'aesthetes' and claimed the public world as their province) seem clumsy amateurs.

Yet Yeats felt he had achieved this conquest without once offending against the Symbolist doctrine that the poet's opinions, his beliefs, his discursive ideas, had no place in poetry. This point requires explanation and illustration.

Responsibilities is the volume in which, as T. S. Eliot has said, Yeats's mature style—'violent and terrible'—is first 'fully evinced'. 'More than half a lifetime', Eliot writes, 'to arrive at this freedom of speech. It is a triumph.'[52] The bitterness which lies behind many of the poems of *Responsibilities* was part of Yeats's long fight with those Irish patriots who had attacked his literary movement for its refusal to accept political verses as poetry. This bitterness intensified in 1907 when Synge was berated because it was thought his plays made fun of the peasantry; it reached its peak in 1913 when the Sinn Fein party opposed Hugh Lane's project for a Dublin Municipal Gallery. Lane had appointed a foreign architect, and was attacked because 'an Irish building should have an Irish architect'.[53] Yeats's poetry was now turned against 'the fumbling wits, the obscure spite' of 'old Paudeen'—his image of materialistic patriotism. Dublin is 'the blind and ignorant town'; its patriots have not 'courage equal to desire'; 'Romantic Ireland's dead and gone':

> 'What need you, being come to sense,
> But fumble in the greasy till,
> And add the halfpence to the pence
> And prayer to shivering prayer until
> You have dried the marrow from the bone?'

The question at once arises: how did Yeats distinguish these poems from the poetry he consistently denounced? Was he making 'out of the quarrel with others rhetoric'? Certainly his Pre-Raphaelite father was alarmed by this new 'freedom of speech'. In 1913 J. B. Yeats wrote to his son:

'I know of old that from the time of your boyhood you have been liable at times, only at times, to a touch of the propaganda fiend—you get it from your father. I like the poetical rhetoric very much—yours and the French—and the Shakespearean rhetoric. But best of all I like the music, when the bird of poesy sings to itself alone in the heart of the wood, persuading and coaxing and commanding and admonishing its own soul, and thinking nothing of others.'[54]

Since we recognize a new authority in these poems of the 1914 volume, and recognize too a difference between their 'rhetoric' and the 'rhetoric' of poets whose work Yeats deplored, his answer to his father's objections is a matter of some interest. His poetry no longer looks like the work of an aesthete; but neither does it resemble in any way the public poems of Kipling, Newbolt, Watson, or their Irish counterparts. These new poems, then, represent some kind of solution of the old antagonism of artist and public man; and Yeats's justification of them offers hints towards an explanation of that solution:

'Of recent years instead of "vision" . . . I have tried for more self-portraiture. I have tried to make my work convincing, with a speech so natural and dramatic that the hearer would feel the presence of man thinking and feeling. . . . Villon always and Ronsard at times create a marvellous drama out of their own lives.'[55]

This explanation was not intensely meaningful to his father,[a] but its idea of poetry as dramatic speech leads directly to Yeats's greatest poems. The terms he uses are at first misleading. 'Self-portraiture', the creation of drama out of one's own life, suggests 'self-expression'. But it must be remembered that for Yeats drama was always stylized—a non-realistic medium: to dramatize himself was not to express his own personality; it was to adopt a persona, to wear a mask. In this he is quite different from Wordsworth, whose poetic persona is inseparable from his personality.

Yeats, like Eliot later, came to believe in the necessary 'impersonality' of poetry, to believe that great poetry defines states of mind more permanent and universal than those conscious thoughts and feelings which are the expression of a single 'personality' in its passage among the accidental and the transient. This 'impersonality'—again in both poets, Yeats and

[a] J. B. Yeats wrote again shortly afterwards, reminding his son 'The chief thing to know and never forget is that art is dreamland . . .' *Letters of J. B. Yeats*, p. 198.

Eliot—is discovered, not outside oneself, but at a level of mind deeper and more obscure than that at which conscious thought and 'opinion' are supreme: at a level where, as Yeats would put it, the mind of the individual becomes the general mind of the race. Thus the persona whose voice is heard in a poem like 'Sailing to Byzantium' is only Yeats to the degree that Prufrock is Eliot —no more. In another poem another voice may embrace the world of dying and generation—the world renounced in 'Sailing to Byzantium'; yet no question of consistency arises, for these are both universal, eternal aspirations of the human mind, different and equally meaningful gestures in the human drama. For the space of one poem the poet commits his energy to the holding of that gesture against the flux of time; the poem does not commit the poet to holding the gesture as a man.

So also, on a level slightly lower than that of his finest achievement, one poem, written in 1913, creates an image of the fervour of patriots as a mean and petty thing; another poem, written in 1916, makes of that fervour something memorable and tragic. 'September 1913' and 'Easter 1916' are choric commentaries on events; neither presents a discursive idea of patriotism; neither asks approval, as a poem on the subject by Kipling or Newbolt would ask it. It is the dramatization of speech, the infusion of life into the speech, which makes Yeats's poems at once impersonal and living, in a world of contemporary events.

With all this in mind we may understand better what Yeats wrote on hearing in 1923 that he was to receive the Nobel Prize for Literature:

'Every now and then, when something has stirred my imagination, I begin talking to myself. I speak in my own person and dramatize myself, very much as I have seen a mad old woman do on the Dublin quays, and sometimes detect myself speaking and moving as if I were still young, or walking perhaps like an old man with fumbling steps. Occasionally, I write out what I have said in verse, and generally for no better reason than because I have written no verse for a long time. I do not think of my soliloquies as having different literary qualities. They stir my interest, by their appropriateness to the men I imagine myself to be, or by their accurate description of some emotional circumstance, more than by any aesthetic value. When I begin to write I have no object but to find for them some natural speech, rhythm and syntax, and to set it out in some pattern, so seeming old that it may seem all men's speech, and though the labour is very great, I seem to have used no faculty peculiar to myself, certainly no special gift. I print the poem and never hear about it again, until I find the book years after with a page dog-eared by some young man, or marked by some young girl with a violet, and when I have seen that, I am a little ashamed, as though someone were to attribute to me a delicacy of feeling I should but do not possess. What came so easily at first, and was written so laboriously at the last, cannot be counted among my possessions.

'On the other hand, if I give a successful lecture, or write a vigorous, critical essay, there is immediate effect; I am confident that on some one point, which seems to me of great importance, I know more than other men, and I covet honour.'[56]

This statement is interesting for more than the description it offers of Yeats assuming the 'mask'. It indicates the degree of 'impersonality' thus attained. The style achieved is always, to the reader, unmistakeably that of Yeats and no other poet, and yet to Yeats himself it seems negative, scarcely of himself at all. The point is made sharper by his contrasting attitude to his critical essays. The essays are discursive expressions of the rational will, of the personality which asserts itself and covets honour. The poems are symbols, or symbolic gestures, that come from a level of mind at which the man is every man, his mind the mind of the race.

'Easter 1916',[57] written to commemorate the 1916 rising against the British occupation of Ireland, is one of the finest of Yeats's public poems. It is a complex poem which, more than illustrating Yeats's achievement of objectivity by means of the dramatic 'mask', uses the terms of drama in order to stylize and objectify the world of political fact which is its subject. In the writing of this poem literary problems have become, for Yeats, analogues for the problems of living: 'Life' and 'Art' interact and merge into a single image.

The first three sections of the poem look backward to a 'comic' world that has been left behind—a world of restless individuality, of mutability, subject to death and re-generation. The fourth section points forward to a world of tragic stasis, achieved by

those killed in the rising. Thus the movement of the poem—
from the temporal to the timeless—and the intermediate
position of Yeats's persona in that movement, make the poem a
forerunner of the more famous 'Sailing to Byzantium'.

The opening lines of the poem present the 'comic' Dublin
scene before the Easter rising:

> 'I have met them at close of day
> Coming with vivid faces
> From counter or desk among grey
> Eighteenth century houses.
> I have passed with a nod of the head
> Or polite meaningless words,
> Or have lingered awhile and said
> Polite meaningless words. . . .'

These, whom Yeats met 'at close of day', are the Irish patriots,
shaped in the world of modern commerce ('from counter or
desk') which came into being with 'grey eighteenth century'
reason. Dublin is part of the civilization that followed when
'the merchant and the clerk,/Breathed on the world with timid
breath'[58]—a fragmented society, where 'polite meaningless
words' serve in place of collective spiritual enterprise. 'Doubt-
less because fragments broke into ever smaller fragments' Yeats
writes in his *Autobiographies* (p. 192), 'we saw one another in
the light of bitter comedy'. The 'vivid faces' of the patriots could
never, it seemed, assume the static mask of tragedy. So the persona of this poem recalls his certainty

> 'that they and I
> But lived where motley is worn.'

But we are warned:

> 'All changed, changed utterly:
> A terrible beauty is born.'

Comedy, Yeats suggests in an essay, accentuates personality,
individual character; tragedy eliminates it in favour of something
universal:

' . . . tragedy must always be a drowning and breaking of the dykes that separate man from man, and . . . it is upon these dykes comedy keeps house. . . .'[59]

The second section of the poem sketches the personalities of some of the nationalists before their destruction in the Easter rising. One, beautiful when young, had spoiled her beauty in the fervour of political agitation; another was a poet and schoolteacher; a third had shown sensitivity and intellectual daring; a fourth had seemed only 'a drunken vainglorious lout'. But the 'dykes that separate man from man' have now been broken. Each has

> 'resigned his part
> In the casual comedy . . .
>
> Transformed utterly:
> A terrible beauty is born.'[a]

So far the change seems all achievement: the petty modern comedy has given way to tragic beauty. But this is also a *terrible beauty*, beauty bought only at the expense of life:

> 'Hearts with one purpose alone
> Through summer and winter seem
> Enchanted to a stone
> To trouble the living stream,
> The horse that comes from the road,
> The rider, the birds that range
> From cloud to tumbling cloud,
> Minute by minute they change;
> A shadow of cloud on the stream
> Changes minute by minute;
> A horse hoof slides on the brim,
> And a horse plashes within it;

a Cf. *Autobiographies*, p. 195: 'I had seen Ireland in my own time turn from the bragging rhetoric and gregarious humour of O'Connell's generation and school, and offer herself to the solitary and proud Parnell as to her anti-self, buskin followed hard on sock . . .'

> The long-legged moor-hens dive,
> And hens to moor-cocks call;
> Minute by minute they live:
> The stone's in the midst of all.'

This third section is a general image of the world subject to time and death ('minute by minute they live')—an image which implies another, kindlier way of seeing the Dublin street before the rising. The nationalists have transcended the mutable word, but only by the destruction of normal human values, by a single-minded-ness that turns the heart to stone. The movement of this section imparts the joy of life, which throws a new light on the 'terrible beauty', emphasizing terror over beauty. The events are thus presented with an ambiguity which does justice to their complexity.

'Nations, races, and individual men', Yeats tells us

'are unified by an image, or bundle or related images, symbolical or evocative of the state of mind which is, of all states of mind not impossible, the most difficult to that man, race or nation; because only the greatest obstacle which can be contemplated without despair rouses the will to full intensity.'[60]

The 'most difficult' image which the nationalists have contemplated 'without despair' is that of a united, independent Ireland. But there is another way of looking at their aspirations:

> 'We had fed the heart on fantasies,
> The heart's grown brutal from the fare;'[61]

Approval and disapproval, delight and disappointment, lie behind the poem. Out of the tensions in Yeats's own mind a complex image is generated. We know from what Maud Gonne has written that Yeats hated in her the passionate intensity that turned the heart to stone.

'Standing by the seashore in Normandy in September 1916 he read me that poem ["Easter 1916"]; he had worked on it all the night before, and he implored me to forget the stone and its inner fire for the flashing, changing joy of life.'[62]

But it was Yeats as a man who urged her to abandon her patriotic
intensity. As a poet his task was more difficult: to make an image
that would encompass the event, transcending mere 'opinion'
—his own, and that of others. To achieve this he must transcend
himself, giving up his personality as the revolutionaries gave up
life, in order to achieve the mask of tragedy. At this level the
writing of the poem becomes an analogue for the event which is
its subject. Yeats is caught up in the play, and must move with
it. He can no longer take pleasure in 'a mocking tale or a gibe'
at the nationalists' expense, for he is no longer 'where motley
is worn'. Nor can he pass judgement: 'That is heaven's part.'
'Our part' is only that of chorus—

> 'our part
> To murmur name upon name,
> As a mother names her child
> When sleep at last has come
> On limbs that had run wild.'

At whatever human expense, a new symbol of heroism has been
created. For good or ill

> 'MacDonagh and MacBride
> And Connolly and Pearse
> Now and in time to be,
> Wherever green is worn,
> Are changed, changed utterly.'

The Irish mind carries a new symbol, and Irish literature a new
poem: there is a new stone resisting the flow of the stream. Such
an achievement constitutes a defeat over the mutable world. The
personalities of principal actors and chorus—of all those whose
interaction created the play—are irrelevant to the effect. The world
is, for the moment in which the event is contemplated, 'transformed utterly'.

Yeats stands alone among English speaking poets of this
century in his ability to assimilate a complex political event into
the framework of a poem without distortion of the event or loss
of its human character in abstraction. It will be worth keeping
'Easter 1916' in mind when we come to consider the English

poets of the First World War. Of them, the patriots are absurdly
partisan, abstract and rhetorical; while the disillusioned soldier
poets—though more admirable than the patriots because their
poems come from honest feeling and particular experience—are
too closely involved in the destruction to be capable of trans-
forming these things, as Yeats transforms them, into a universal
image. It is—in terms of the metaphor I have used in my Introduction—a matter of establishing a correct distance between the
poet and his subject. The soldier poets stand too close to their
subject, the patriots at too great a distance. Yeats's dramatic
'mask' is a means of holding himself at a correct distance.[a] He
had pored long enough over the slow fires of his own and others'
art, to know that death in itself is a commonplace; but that
particular death, transformed in poetry to an object of contemplation, becomes a symbol—a way of understanding and expressing the human condition.

In 'Easter 1916' Yeats has already achieved a solution—one
solution—to a problem which had bedeviled poetry for many
years: the problem of how a poem could enter the public world
without losing itself in temporal 'opinion'. 'Easter 1916' is not a
pure Symbolist poem, for it is capable of discursive paraphrase;
but no paraphrase can use up the poem's life. The event which is
its subject is not described, but re-fashioned. There is no question
of simply praising heroism or blaming folly. The men of the poem
are all dead—'all changed, changed utterly'—no longer men at
all but symbols that take life in the mind. Yeats leaves his
personality, his opinions, behind. He puts on the mask of tragic
chorus, and out of the slow impersonal contemplation of a
particular event in which idealism, folly, heroism, and destruc-
tiveness were intermixed, fashions an image which stands for
all such events in human history.

a Cf. Yeats writing of two of his contemporary poets in *The Boston
Pilot*, 23 April 1892. 'The din and glitter one feels were far too near the
writer [John Davidson]. He has not been able to cast them back into
imaginative dimness and distance. Of Mr Symons' method . . . I have
but seen stray poems and judge from them that, despite most manifest
triumphs from time to time, he will sometimes fail through gaining too
easily that very dimness and distance I have spoken of. He will, perhaps,
prove to be too far from, as Mr Davidson is too near to, his subject.'
Letters to The New Island, p. 147.

3. The equilateral triangle

In this brief survey up to the year 1916, Yeats is observed adjusting the distance on the one hand between himself and his audience, on the other between himself and the particular area of experience which is the subject of his poetry. The difficulty of this adjustment is perhaps best illustrated by the reaction of the Irish nationalists to 'Easter 1916'. They—Maud Gonne among them—considered the poem inadequate to the occasion. One imagines they did not enjoy finding themselves, together with the event, pushed back to a point at which Yeats could regard them, not with the eye of a partisan, but with an eye 'cold/And passionate as the dawn'. In this sense 'Easter 1916' is written for

> 'A man who does not exist,
> A man who is but a dream.'

Maud Gonne's judgement on Yeats is the judgement of a partisan, and a partisan could never appreciate fully an achievement which demanded freedom from temporal commitment:

> 'Yeats's aloofness and his intolerance of mediocrity, a spiritual pride which is dangerous, tended to keep him apart from the first person of the National Trinity, the People.'[63]

What she did not add, because it was something she could not know, was that the greatness of Yeats's poetry depended on this separateness—not a total separation, but a correct distance.

As his style hardened towards maturity Yeats lost many of his early sentimental admirers; for these, *Responsibilities* can have seemed only the beginning of a long decline into the obscurity of 'modernism'. 'There is nothing which can be put beside the "Isle of Innisfree" ' the *Athenaeum* declared:[64]

> 'Still it must be remembered that these poems, unless we are much mistaken, represent a period in the poet's life when the flush of faery inspiration to which we owe "The Wind Among

the Reeds", "Rose of all Roses", "To Ireland in the Coming Times', and other lyrics even more beautiful than "Innisfree", had given place to a pressure of lectures in America, stage managing at the Abbey Theatre, the social life in London and Paris, and other distractions of, shall we say, middle age?—which may well have drawn Mr Yeats away from his beloved seven woods.'

As he lost his old admirers, however, Yeats acquired new ones, whose more adequate praise he preferred to ill-founded popularity. In 1915 he wrote to a reviewer:

'One great pleasure is that whereas I used to feel that the articles people wrote in praise of my early work were, with some few exceptions, vague and a little sentimental, the very few who praise the later work . . . have praised it in words full of intellect and force. That convinces me, that and my own emotion when I write, that I am doing better and plunging deeper.'[65]

Ezra Pound was one of those who were quick to praise the new work. In the May 1914 issue of *Poetry* he commended Yeats for 'seeking greater hardness of outline', and praised the achievement of a new 'quality of hard light' in the poems:

' . . . a lot of his admirers will be displeased with this book. That is always a gain for the poet, for his admirers always want him to "stay put", and they resent any signs of stirring, of new curiosity or of intellectual uneasiness.'

Events in the literary world, then, were moving with Yeats. In the next two chapters I shall shift the focus of my attention to the literary scene during the years 1909 to 1916—the years in which the most significant changes in Yeats's poetry are observed —to discover whether the new poets appearing at this time felt themselves faced with the problems Yeats had faced. In Chapter 3 I shall discuss the various attempts made by these new poets to adjust the distance between themselves and their audience; and in Chapter 4, the relationship at this time between 'Poetry' and 'Life'.

REFERENCES

1. *Autobiographies*, 1955, p. 318.
2. *Essays*, 1961, pp. 223 and 227.
3. ibid., p. 318.
4. *Ideas of Good and Evil*, 1903, pp. 3, 4.
5. *Letters of W. B. Yeats*, edited by A. Wade, 1954, p. 880.
6. *Oxford Book of Modern Verse*, edited by W. B. Yeats, 1935. Introduction, p. ix.
7. Quoted by A. N. Jeffares, *W. B. Yeats, Man and Poet*, pp. 91–2.
8. ibid., p. 92.
9. *Ideas of Good and Evil*, p. 320.
10. ibid., p. 6.
11. ibid., p. 254.
12. ibid., p. 10.
13. ibid., p. 258.
14. ibid., p. 337.
15. ibid., p. 338.
16. ibid., p. 327.
17. *Autobiographies*, p. 120.
18. *Essays*, 1961, p. 250.
19. ibid., p. 251.
20. ibid., p. 265.
21. ibid., p. 266.
22. ibid., p. 272. Italics mine.
23. ibid., p. 349 ('Art and Ideas' 1913).
24. *Letters*, p. 768.
25. 1909 Diary, quoted Jeffares, op. cit., p. 141.
26. *Essays*, 1961, p. 238.
27. 'Meditations in Time of Civil War', *Collected Poems*, p. 232.
28. *Letters*, p. 807.
29. ibid., p. 610.
30. ibid., p. 652.
31. ibid., p. 873.
32. *Autobiographies*, p. 494.
33. 'To Ireland in the Coming Times', *Collected Poems*, p. 56.
34. *Ideas of Good and Evil*, p. 7.
35. *Autobiographies*, p. 300.
36. *Ideas of Good and Evil*, p. 240.
37. *Autobiographies*, p. 313.
38. *Letters*, p. 672.
39. *Samhain*, quoted by J. Hone, *W. B. Yeats 1865–1939*, 1949, p. 194.
40. *Essays*, 1961, pp. 256–7.

41. 'Per Amica Silentia Lunae' (1917), *Mythologies*, 1959, p. 343.
42. *Selected Essays*, p. 320.
43. *Essays*, 1961, p. 348.
44. *Autobiographies*, p. 493.
45. ibid., p. 567.
46. 'Responsibilities', 1914, *Collected Poems*, p. 113.
47. *Romantic Image*, 1957, p. 5.
48. ibid., p. 47.
49. ibid., p. 11.
50. 'Per Amica Silentia Lunae' (1917), *Mythologies*, 1959, p. 331.
51. ibid., p. 334.
52. *Selected Prose* (Penguin), 1953, p. 202.
53. *The Letters of W. B. Yeats*, p. 591.
54. *Letters of J. B. Yeats*, edited by J. Hone, 1944, p. 168.
55. *Letters*, p. 583.
56. *Autobiographies*, pp. 532–3.
57. *Collected Poems*, p. 202.
58. 'At Galway Races', *Collected Poems*, p. 108.
59. *Essays*, 1961, p. 241.
60. *Autobiographies*, p. 194.
61. 'Meditations in Time of Civil War', *Collected Poems*, p. 230.
62. *Scattering Branches, Tributes to the Memory of W. B. Yeats*, edited by Stephen Gwynn, 1940, pp. 31–2.
63. ibid., p. 27.
64. November 1916, p. 529.
65. *Letters*, p. 593.

3

1909–16: POETS AND THEIR PUBLIC

Sonority . . . like a goose

'The situation of poetry in 1909 or 1910 was stagnant to
a degree difficult for any young poet of today to imagine.'

T. S. ELIOT[1]

'And even this infamy would not attract numerous readers
Were there an erudite or violent passion,
For the nobleness of the populace brooks nothing below
    its own altitude.
One must have resonance, resonance and sonority . . . like
    a goose.'

EZRA POUND[2]

YEATS's attitude to 'the public' during the early years of this century shows what may seem at this distance an unnecessary caution, an inordinate fear of corruption by popularity. It may seem that he was surprisingly slow to break free of the doctrines of the 'nineties, and that his refusal to acknowledge the presence of a middle-class audience was only part of a larger self-deception —his 'dream of the noble and the beggarman'. A close look at the literary situation in England in the early years of this century, however, makes it clear that Yeats was defending himself against something real. The caution with which he went about broadening the scope of his poetry shows an accurate awareness of the dangers involved at this time in any direct acknowledgement of a living two-way relationship between poet and audience.

In the literary journalism of the time one finds constant reference to 'the public', and it is necessary first to consider what this

term implies. Arnold Bennett, a writer who approached his work
in a hard-headed and clear-sighted fashion, assessed in 1909 the
size and quality of the audience whose attention provided him
with a living:

'The crowd I see in these [bookshops] is the prosperous crowd,
the crowd which grumbles at income tax and pays it. Three
hundred and seventy-five thousand persons paid income tax
last year under protest: they stand for the existence of perhaps
a million souls, and this million is a handful floating more or
less easily on the surface of the forty millions of the population.
The greatest majority of my readers must be somewhere in this
million . . . I see at the counters people on whose foreheads it is
written that they know themselves to be the salt of the earth.
Their assured, curt voices, their proud carriage, their clothes,
the similarity of their manners, all show that they belong to a
caste and that the caste has been successful in the struggle for
life.'[3]

The literary taste of most of these readers was established by the
writings of a small group of reviewers in a few influential papers.
Ford Madox Ford considers that the damage done to literature
by the literary pages of the *Daily Telegraph*, for example, was
incalaculable:

'It heralded mediocrity to the sound of shawms and oboes:
it never praised any writer of merit and originality until he had
grown old and imbecile. Its influence among the middle classes
was tremendous. The manager of Mudie's circulating library
told me that every Friday at lunchtime he was inundated by the
warmer inhabitants of the Square Mile. These chief city-men
of the Empire would remove their silk hats. Inside the leather
linings their careful spouses would have placed the list of books
they desired to read during the ensuing week. Almost invariably
these lists consisted of a clipping from the *Daily Telegraph*.'[4]

A 'popular' poet or 'popular' novelist in the year 1909 meant a
poet or novelist widely read among the group of readers described by Arnold Bennett, and to be popular among these readers
required either conformity to their conventions of thought and

behaviour, or at least avoidance of open violation of those conventions. Bennett gives an irascible account of the characteristics shared by the members of this class:

'Another marked characteristic is its gigantic temperamental dullness, unresponsiveness to external suggestion, a lack of humour—in short a heavy and half honest stupidity: ultimate product of gross prosperity . . . Then I notice a grim passion for the *status quo*. . . . This passion shows itself in a naive admiration for everything that has survived its original usefulness, such as saildrill and uniforms. . . . The passion for the *status quo* also shows itself in a general defensive, sullen hatred of all ideas whatever. You cannot argue with these people.'[5]

One cannot read long among the established reputations of this period without accepting Bennett's description—at least as a justifiable reaction. In English society during the early years of this century it was inevitable that any widely popular writer was either bad—that is, that he shared the 'gigantic temperamental dullness' of his audience—or that his works were in some way a compromise. Bennett himself, perhaps because he was not a writer of the first rank, accepted the compromise. He was fully aware of what he was doing. His intention, if we can believe F. M. Ford, was to get £40,000 into his own bank account, and until that was done every other consideration was of secondary importance. Henry James, on the other hand, was 'hardly known of by the general public' and 'Mr Yeats was known as having written "The Lake Isle of Innisfree" '.[6]

In one of the articles he wrote during 1909 Bennett quotes, as an example of an attitude to literature common at the time, a letter from a publisher to a young author:

'Get down to the facts, my son, and study your market. Find out what people like to read and then write a story along those lines. This will bring you success . . . Remember that novel writing is as much a business as making calico.'[7]

Bennett aptly ridicules this letter; yet by 1913 he was warning about 'the futility of writing what will not be immediately read', and arguing that 'the sagacious artist will respect basic national

prejudices'.[8] We can only now be grateful for the lack of 'sagacity'
Pound, Eliot, and Joyce were manifesting in that year; and
especially for Pound's efforts, on behalf of the other two, to ensure
that 'what would not be immediately read' was at least printed.

It is likely, then, that Mr Hugh Kenner is correct when he
suggests that Ezra Pound's Mr Nixon in *Hugh Selwyn Mauberley*
is Bennett. Mr Nixon is made by Pound to typify the corruption
of literary compromise in pre-war London:

> 'In the cream gilded cabin of his steam yacht
>   Mr Nixon advised me kindly, to advance with fewer
>   Dangers of delay.   "Consider
>   Carefully the reviewer.
> "I was as poor as you are:
> "When I began I got, of course,
> "Advance on royalties, fifty at first," said Mr Nixon,
> "Follow me, and take a column,
> "Even if you have to work free.
> "Butter reviewers. From fifty to three hundred
> "I rose in eighteen months;
> "The hardest nut I had to crack
> "Was Dr Dundas.
> "I never mentioned a man but with the view
> "Of selling my own works.
> "The tip's a good one, as for literature
> "It gives no man a sinecure.
> "And no one knows, at sight, a masterpiece.
> "And give up verse, my boy,
> "There's nothing in it." '[9]

A society in which literature is ignored, except by a tiny
minority, is unpromising enough. But one in which a traditional
respect for literature is mixed with narrow demands for poetry
and novels of a particular, second-rate kind is worse. The 'great'
names of poetry in England during the first decade of this century
are now either forgotten or neglected. But they are worth
examination if only to shed light on what may now seem an
unnecessary violence and waywardness in the prose writings of
genuine poets like Pound and Yeats. Bennett's 1909 analysis of
the literary public continues:

'Lastly I am impressed by their attitude towards the artist, which is medieval, or perhaps Roman. Blind to every form of beauty, they scorn art, and scorning art they scorn artists . . . Only sheer ennui drives [this class] to seek distraction in the artist's work. It prefers the novelists among artists because the novel gives the longest surcease from boredom.'[10]

The popular poets, then, were not those who offered the complex qualities usually associated with good poetry, but those whose minds ran at the level of public expectation. Poetry was acceptable when it effectively versified Imperialist sentiments, the public school spirit, or patriotic fervour: otherwise it was unlikely to be widely read. The result was a low-charged literary atmosphere in which second-rate men grotesquely assumed the mannerisms considered appropriate to the position of public bard. And with this 'debasement of the literary coin'[11] went an almost total elimination of active criticism. 'The general tendency of British criticism at the time', Pound says,[12] 'was towards utter petrification or vitrefaction, and Henry Newbolt was as good an example of the best *accepted* criteria as can be unearthed.' Thus one of the great 'names' in English poetry of the day (Maurice Hewlett) could write to another, more important (Henry Newbolt), praising the latter's new book—

'There's only one word for it: Ripping! I envy you many things—but chiefly two: your lyre and your piety.'[13]

The frustration of the genuine poet in such a milieu is exemplified in the conversation which Pound records as 'evidence of the state of mind among the English letterati' of the time:

'*Hewlett* in praise of Newbolt likens N's work to "the Ballads".
E.P.: But . . . (blanks for profanity) . . . it,
Hewlett, look at the line:
He stood the door behind
(blanks for profanity) you don't find lines
like that in Patrick Spens.
Hewlett: But, but I don't mean an OLDE ballad,
I mean an eh—eighteenth century ballad.

E.P.: But (blanks for profanity) Hewlett, the
  man is a contemporary of Rémy de Gourmont!
Hewlett: Ungh!! Unh nnh, eh, I don't suppose he
  has thought of that. (Long pause)
Hewlett (continues very slowly): I don't
  suppose, eh, I had either.'[14]

A man like Pound could make little or no impression on this
closed, self-satisfied community resting comfortably on the crest
of years of peace and prosperity, and confident that nothing from
'outside' itself could offer anything of value. Newbolt continued
to remind public schoolboys of their duty to

'Play up, play up, and play the game!'

Kipling encouraged his countrymen to

'Take up the white man's burden;'

William Watson, eyeing the Turks unfavourably, addressed his
motherland as the scourge of God:

'How long shall they be born, O England? Up,
  Tempest of God, and sweep them to their doom!'

While Alfred Noyes provided every Englishman with an ideal
image of himself:

'A voice
Rough with the storms of many an ocean called,
"Drake! Cap'en Drake! The Armada. In the Channel!"
All eyes were turned on Drake, as he stood there,
Looming against the sunset and the sea,
Stiller than bronze. Far off, the first white star
Gleamed as if motionless in heaven, a world
Of lonely light and 'wildering speed.
                            He tossed
A grim black ball in the lustrous air and laughed—
"Come lads," he said, "we've time to finish the game." '

But perhaps the best illustration of the level to which poetry had sunk is the image Newbolt uses to represent death in his poem 'The Best School of All':

> 'We'll honour yet the school we knew
>   The best school of all;
> We'll honour yet the rule we knew
>   Till the last bell call.'

If one considers that men were not only acclaimed for such lines, but made a living by writing them, one must concede the justness of Bennett's analysis of the reading public. An example of the 'gigantic temperamental dullness', the 'lack of humour', the 'heavy and half honest stupidity' which Bennett describes can be found in a letter to Newbolt from an old Cliftonian friend:

'I have the greatest possible faith in our race and in its high destiny: but we won't reach that high destiny without strenuous work, persistency of purpose and constant watchfulness . . . I want especially to devote myself to defining our true position and role among the nations. . . . The Empire *must* grow; we cannot help it. But we can in some degree direct that growth, and more important still we can see that our organization keeps pace with our growth. I have not much experience of the organization of our white population and of the binding together of the Mother Country and the Colonies. But I have some experience in the organization of our Asiatic subjects, and that training I hope I may be able to make especially useful to our own country. I believe our position in the world will depend upon how we lead and attach to us these weaker races of Asia and Africa who have fallen and will fall within the sphere of our control.

'The greatest question which lies before us at present is the Chinese Question, and the solution of that depends on the use we make of India and of our genius for leading the Asiatics . . .'[15]

Newbolt's comment on this letter was that as an Imperialist 'a little sensitive about the views and utterances of my fellow Imperialists', he welcomed it as 'a really sane opinion'. The intentions expressed are, of course, honourable enough; but a man like Newbolt could never see the degree to which, in such generalized and emotional statements, the facts of Britain's role in the world were distorted by feeling. (In this context it is worth recalling the brilliant note, 'A Romantic Aristocrat',[16] in which T. S. Eliot discusses how literature suffers when it serves a romantically conceived imperialism.)

This image of Englishmen 'drawing up with [them] these hundred of millions' of their 'Asiatic subjects'[17], is common in the poetry of the time. Thus William Watson addresses English politicians of the day in a rhetoric which mixes images of power with the heavy rhythms of responsibility:

> 'You in high places; you that drive the steeds
> Of Empire; you that say unto your hosts,
> "Go thither", and they go; and from our coasts
> Bid sail the squadrons, and they sail, their deeds
> Shaking the world . . .'

This was the kind of poetry widely read—a poetry, as Yeats says, 'which was always tending to lose itself in externalities of all kinds, in opinion, in declamation, in picturesque writing'.[18] And it was to poetry of this kind that publishers and editors gave support, ultimately 'debasing the literary coin to a point where it no longer deceives even the gulls'.[19]

Another group to be considered in the pre-war literary scene was the horde of amateurs writing and publishing imitations of the five or six poets with large reputations. These amateurs set the standards by which new writers were accepted as worthy of attention. 'London swarms', Bennett wrote in 1910,

'with the dilettanti of letters. They do not belong to the criminal class, but their good intentions, their culture, their judiciousness, and their infernal cheek amount perhaps to worse than arson or assault. . . . The Press is their washpot. And they are influential in other places. They can get pensions for their favourites. . . . In every generation they select some artist, usually for reasons quite unconnected with art, and put him exceedingly high up in a niche by himself. And when you name his name you must hush your voice, and discussion ends.'[20]

The presence of this group throws further light on the arrogance and occasional violence of Yeats and Pound for whom the writing of good poetry was something requiring the concentration of a lifetime. The aim was perfection. The response of the dilettanti to this attitude is described by Wyndham Lewis:

'The word perfection . . . has obvious professional associations . . . "It is impossible" Pound wrote "to talk about perfection without getting yourself much disliked. It is even more difficult in a capital where everybody's Aunt Lucy or Uncle George has written something-or-other." . . .

'A huge rentier army of the intellectual or the artistic emerged, like a cloud of locusts, from the Victorian Age, and it covered the entire landscape, to the dismay of the authentic artist. They drifted dreamily out, paint-brush in hand, or with novelist's notebook tucked away in their overcoat pocket, choking professional talent—drawing all the applause to themselves, as Pound indicates, because they were such awfully nice people (and the critics were not looking for artistic perfection, but social *niceness*). This lifeless host of niceness eyed Pound, very naturally, askance. A *professional!* Hum! But that of course was what was the matter with Americans! They took their sports seriously.'[21]

The year 1909 marks perhaps the lowest point of a long decline in the quality of English poetry. The 'aesthetic' movement of the 'nineties had long since collapsed with the trial of Wilde when, as F. M. Ford puts it, 'Poets died or fled to other climes, publishers also fled, prosateurs were fished out of the Seine or reformed and the great public said "Thank heavens, we need not read any more poetry" '.[22] The work of the aesthetes had been replaced by that of what Ford calls 'the physical force school', a change which corresponded with a violent swing of the political pendulum to the Right.[23]

In April 1909 Swinburne died, and in May, George Meredith. In June the *English Review* commented:

'Mr Meredith follows Mr Swinburne into the shadows; and now indeed the whole Round Table is dissolved.'

Yeats hearing the news remarked: 'And now I am king of the cats.' In the same year he published his *Collected Poems*, and there were new volumes by Kipling, Noyes, Watson, and Newbolt. The English poetic scene offered a rather spiritless Yeats, and a collection of public-spirited versifiers.

Yet 1909 can also be seen as a year carrying the beginnings, unrecognized at the time, of what we now acknowledge to be a resurgence of poetry in the twentieth century. Yeats's collected poems of that year put an outworn style and restricted sensibility behind him, making way for the new, more robust poetry that was soon to emerge. In the same year the Imagist movement was first formed, Pound's *Personae* appeared, and a valuable association between Pound and Yeats was formed. The earliest of Eliot's published poems were also written in 1909, though they were not printed until 1915. These events mark the beginnings of a movement in English poetry which by 1930 had succeeded in establishing that it was the poet's task first to write good poems, and only his second task to please an audience. But in 1909 the future was well hidden; and the gulf between the genuine poet (as opposed to those who offered the public a reflection of its own generalized emotions) and the reading public is indicated in Arnold Bennett's comments on the death of Swinburne:

'When Tennyson died, everybody knew it, and imaginatively realized it. I was saddened then as much by the contagion of a general grief as by a sorrow of my own. But there was no general grief on Saturday. Swinburne had written for fifty years and never once moved the nation, save inimically, when "Poems and Ballads" came near to being burned publicly by the hangman. (By "nation" I mean newspaper readers. The real nation, busy with the problems of eating, dying, and being born all in one room, has never heard of Tennyson or Swinburne or George R. Sims.) There are poems of Tennyson, Wordsworth, even of the speciously recondite Browning, that have entered into the general consciousness. But nothing of Swinburne's. Swinburne never publicly yearned to meet his Pilot face to face. He never galloped on one of Lord George Sanger's horses from Aix to Ghent. He was interested only in ideal manifestations of beauty and force. Except when he grieved the judicious by the expression of political crudities, he never connected art with any form of morals that the British public could understand. He sang. He sang supremely. And it wasn't enough for the British public.'[24]

Reading issues of the *Times Literary Supplement* for 1909 one receives a double image: the image of the state of poetry as it was presented to the literary public of the time; and the quite contrary image of that situation as we see it now with almost every literary valuation turned on its head. The situation for poetry is presented optimistically, almost gaily. A reviewer writes:

' . . . we may say boldly that poetry is being cultivated at the present day with an energy, a varied range of emotion, and a technical skill of which we may be proud. Year after year new writers come forward with new verse. Year after year there are new aims, new developments, or (what may be just as original) new reactions. No one can move exactly on old lines. No one finds that what he wishes has been said in exactly the way he wishes to say it. There is no universal model, no acclaimed or accredited school. Everyone is free to use the manner that suits him, with nothing to fear from academic criticism. And in this favouring atmosphere fresh experiments succeed each other so rapidly that it is hardly possible at one moment to say what the dominant note of the next moment will be.'[25]

This picture of freedom and unimpeded literary activity is not borne out by further reading of the same paper. When the established poets are reviewed they are not only praised in words which had become meaningless through overuse in the previous century, but in a tone which suggests that any other approach to poetry is undesirable. A review of new books by William Watson, Alfred Noyes, and Henry Newbolt begins:

'The three poets whose names are here joined, different as they are from each other, are alike in this, that they all belong to the centre of poetical tradition. Neither [sic] of them insists on any new formula for the definition of poetry. The compass of the old instrument is, in their view, still wide enough to contain modern music. They aim at a quality of beauty in expression which demands no violent readjustment of sympathy or taste on the part of the reader.'[26]

More obscurely still, the reviewer goes on to praise Newbolt by arguing that his new poems 'probably mark the highest level which Mr Newbolt's poetry has yet touched. They certainly show the rare art, the art that seems to be more attainable in music than in poetry, of sustaining deliberate and even devious thought in the purely lyric mood.'

The established poets receive full-length reviews, in which they are invariably praised for the quality of 'beauty' their poetry displays. In the same year Ezra Pound's *Personae* is dismissed in a few lines for lacking this quality. The full review reads:

'Ezra Pound admires Browning, whom he addresses as "old Hippety-hop o' the accents". Like Browning he is fond of medieval and Latin themes, and he affects the eccentric and the obscure; but these qualities do not, in these pages at any rate, leave much room for beauty.'[27]

'There is no town like London', Pound wrote in a letter, 'to make one feel the vanity of all art except the highest. To make one disbelieve in all but the most careful and conservative presentation of one's stuff'.[28] But his essential seriousness was to remain unrecognized during what he called 'eight years hammering against the impenetrable adamant'.[29]

The depressed state of poetry in England in 1909 was little altered by its few saving factors. F. M. Ford's editorship of the *English Review*, for example, despite its brilliant beginning in that year, and Ford's intention of providing a venue for the better writers who had little success with the established periodicals, lasted only briefly. No sooner had Ford established his periodical than it was taken out of his hands, and thereafter its quality rapidly declined. Edward Marsh, however, being independent financially, was more secure in his editorial ventures; and the appearance of his first *Georgian Anthology* in 1912 represents the first significant change in a literary scene otherwise virtually static.

The Georgians have been severely criticized during the past thirty years, and the fashion of treating them as representatives of reaction in poetry has obscured the good service their appearance did. More will be said about this in Chapter 4; but it is important to record here that in 1912 many of the younger

Georgian poets were considered dangerous literary revolutionaries. Edward Marsh in fact turned his back on the established
names of the day in an attempt to show the reading public that
a more genuine poetry was being written. He criticized his
young protégés when they used the outmoded diction common in
poetry at the time; and he was generally regarded as a daring
innovator.[30]

The view of Marsh as an innovator may seem strange at this
date, but it is not strange when one considers his choice of poets
in relation to the accepted standards of the time. D. H. Lawrence,
in a poem like 'The Snapdragon'[31] for example, exercised that
'freedom in treating sexual phenomena' which Arnold Bennett
argued the English reading public would not tolerate. Rupert
Brooke committed an act of literary vandalism when he wrote
about sea-sickness; and he was known to his literary seniors
as 'a frank polygamist, and rather cynical about it'.[32] John
Masefield was thought to be a technical innovator. And later the
Georgian Anthology housed a number of war poets whose work
was considered by writers like Newbolt (who also described
Wilfred Owen's disgust as 'hardly normal'[33]) to be a kind of
literary insubordination.

The Georgians, however, never adopted the attitude which
Pound and the Imagists found to be essential if they were to
remain free of hampering influences—the attitude which insisted
'the public can go to the devil'.[34] Theirs was an attempt to educate
public taste rather than to dismiss the reading public as too
degenerate in taste to deserve consideration. In this respect
Harold Monro was the most active of them:

'It is said that he was lamenting the state of English poetry
before Max Beerbohm or some other votary of the red lily when
Beerbohm or the other exclaimed: "If you feel like that why on
earth don't you go back to England and do something?" Monro
went and did something; he spent the rest of his life and a great
deal of his money doing it.'[35]

Monro set up the Poetry Bookshop, a London centre for the
publication as well as the sale of poetry. Only poetry was sold,
and all poetry published was available. At the back of the shop
was a barn in which poetry readings were organized and an

immediate contact between the poet and his audience could be established. Upstairs there were rooms where poets could sleep or write. (It was comforting to think, an American journalist commented, that while you were buying a book down below, the poetry factory was in full blast above.) In March 1913 Monro began editing *Poetry and Drama*, and later he organized the monthly *Chapbook* series. 'He did more', F. S. Flint comments, 'to stir up an interest in poetry than any other man of his generation.'[36]

Yet Monro is interesting in some ways because he represents the Georgian 'middle course' which in the existing literary situation could never be successful. He retained a faith that poetry could be widely popular, and a belief that it *ought* to be popular, at a time when such revolutionary changes were needed that the poet could only write well by flouting public opinion or at least by disappointing public expectation. Some of the Georgians' confusion in facing their public can be illustrated by Monro's commentaries in *Poetry and Drama*:

'A majority of intelligent people [he writes] still argues that poetry is unpopular: it is one of the objects of *Poetry and Drama* to dispel this illusion. . . . The appreciation of civilized poetry requires study, and study requires effort; therefore most people placidly and very deliberately leave poetry alone.'[37]

At this point he has admitted that poetry goes mainly unread, which is not at all what he wants to emphasize. He therefore continues:

'That is not to say they dislike it. A good song pleases people; a bad one leaves them indifferent or angry. . . . Shakespeare wrote for the great public, Goethe too, and probably also Homer. The bad popular poet . . . such as Tennyson, Lewis Morris, or Kipling, is bad because he studies what the public likes instead of forcing it to like what he may choose to give it.'

He has now reached a point at which both the best and the worst poets he can think of are popular; yet it is neither group that he has in mind. He continues

'If we could agree . . . that poetry is unpopular, we should add that the average poet has made it so.'

As the representative of a group of poets who were making no claims to greatness, this seems undiplomatic. The original claim (which makes the point of the whole article again obscure) is therefore repeated:

'But poetry is not unpopular.'

This article illustrates the bewilderment of men brought up in the tradition of nineteenth-century respect for poetry as a public ornament, and yet conscious that the kind of ornaments demanded by the public were seldom of a kind the poet himself wished to make. Nevertheless Monro did a great deal of good work by helping groups like the Imagists (whom he published) even when he disagreed with their revolutionary principles;[a] and by waging a constant war on bad taste in poetry. In June 1913, for example, he criticizes the misrepresentation by publishers of a book of very bad verse which has gone into four editions:

'At a time when certain genuine attempts are being made to bring a wider public to a true appreciation of poetry, not by *vulgarization*, but by putting all that is best before it and trusting to its right perception, we feel that we cannot too strongly condemn this commercial engineering of the market, which constitutes a mischievous misrepresentation and a wilful degradation of art.'[38]

In another issue[39] he attacks the *English Review* for publishing bad verse:

'We would remind the *English Review* of the public responsibility of its reputation, and would suggest that it would be better not to print any poetry at all than to approach a wavering public with verses which may disgust it into withdrawing its attention from the real poetry of modern England.'

  a Pound to Hariet Monroe, September 1915: 'Monro discovered "Prufrock" on his unaided own and asked me about the author when I saw him last night'. Pound, *Letters*, p. 108.

One notices that both these attacks are founded on a belief that the public will respond if it is offered poetry of a reasonable standard, and if its tastes have not already been corrupted by the middle-men of literature—editors, publishers, critics. In March 1914 the conduct of poetry reviewing is criticized in a comment which throws light on the level of critical integrity common at the time:

'Is it I wonder a revelation to anyone that in the majority of editorial offices preference is given to books whose publishers are advertisers in the paper, that favour is shown to friends and partisans of the paper, colleagues in trade and great reputations that must not be impunged, that insipid critics are preferred so long as they have two or three hundred cliché phrases at their command, or tired critics, sometimes too tired to object to writing what they are told? Their sentences are quoted as "Opinions of the Press". Reputations are made like those of William Watson or Alfred Noyes. . . . The criticism of poetry has been prostituted out of all recognition: it still remains genuine in only a few periodicals.'[40]

Poetry and Drama was not the only sign of new life at this time. The *Blue Review* (run by John Middleton Murry, Katherine Mansfield, and D. H. Lawrence) ran concurrently with it for a short time. And by late 1913 the lady editor of the *New Free-woman* (a periodical devoted to women's suffrage and the place of women in modern society) had been bullied by Ezra Pound into changing the title of her paper to the *Egoist* and devoting most of its pages to the writings of the Imagist poets.

In the face of this solid and serious-minded opposition, the organs of literary conservatism were forced to defend themselves. One such, the *Poetry Review* (official journal of the Poetry Society) from which Harold Monro had broken away to edit *Poetry and Drama*, expressed its confidence in itself in a tone which it would not have needed to adopt two or three years earlier:

'That wider public, unaffected by the querulous bleat of the neglected poetaster-turned-critic and indifferent to the jealous attacks of immaturity on established reputations has been reached; that "large, scattered body of cultivated, intelligent,

serious, but silent lovers of fine literature, who are quite un-
swayed by literary fashions" of whom Mr Watson speaks,
recognize that the *Poetry Review* appeals to and represents them,
and is not the mouthpiece of a coterie, superior or otherwise.
Our latest subscribers are symbolical—a police constable and a
Peer, a University Professor and an elementary school teacher,
a country vicar and a suburban doctor. Our readers are as catholic as our policy, and we believe that with our freedom from
narrowing influences and captious intolerance, from the petty
vanities of exotic youth and the ennervating influences of the
log-roller, they will increase still more rapidly, bound to us by
the golden chains of sane and sincere appreciation. We realize
the responsibilities of a journal of world-wide repute, quoted
in Sydney and Winnipeg, London and Chicago, and are determined to be steadfast to our trust.'[41]

Alfred Noyes declared publicly that the poets who read at the
Poetry Bookshop (one of whom was Yeats) were 'bringing the
contempt of the man in the street down on poetry'.[42] William
Watson complained that 'Certain of our Georgian singers . . .
are so haunted by a dread of smoothness that they have very
nearly erected cacophony into a cult. They pursue it as an end
in itself laudable'.[43] While the *Quarterly Review* bracketed the
first two Georgian anthologies with Pound's *Catholic Anthology*
(in which T. S. Eliot appeared) and discussed them as 'the new
rebellion'.[a]

This last-mentioned article is worth quoting because it probably
illustrates a common first reaction to the Georgians among a
public conditioned to the work of Kipling, Newbolt, and Noyes:

'Now a careful examination of these two volumes of Georgian
poetry seems to suggest that during the last ten years or so

a 'The New Poetry', Arthur Waugh, October 1916. Ezra Pound was
not writing strict truth when he accused this reviewer (in the *Egoist*,
June 1917) of calling T. S. Eliot 'a drunken helot'—a story which
Eliot repeats in *The Use of Poetry* . . . (p. 71). Waugh did, however,
suggest that there was a warning to be taken from the appearance
of the *Catholic Anthology* which might be compared with that intended
in Sparta when the drunken helot was displayed: the warning that
'emancipation' and 'licence' lead to 'anarchy'.

English poetry has been approaching a condition of liberty and licence which threatens, not only to submerge old standards altogether, but, if persevered in to its logical limits, to hand over the sensitive art of verse to a general process of literary democratisation.'

The reviewer goes on to describe Georgian poetry as 'an unrestrained and even violent fashion'; to insist that a return to natural speech in poetry can only produce 'a fitful lack of dignity'; and to attack D. H. Lawrence's poems as representing 'a degree of self-abandonment which is so invertebrate as to be practically abnormal'. Finally the Georgians are dismissed in the traditional manner:

' . . . in their determination to surprise and even to puzzle at all costs, these young poets are forgetting that the first essence of poetry is beauty; and that, however much you have observed the world around you, it is impossible to translate your observation into poetry, without the intervention of the spirit of beauty . . .'

Until the war the new movements did not succeed in catching the attention of the public. The old favourites remained. In 1913 the *Journal of Education* held a plebiscite to discover the most popular poets in England, still living. Kipling received twice as many votes as his nearest rival, William Watson. Robert Bridges (not the same kind of poet, but one whose diction was recognizably 'beautiful') was third. Alfred Noyes was fourth. In addition to these men who had dominated English poetry for fifteen years, the 'cloud of locusts' described by Wyndham Lewis still obscured the literary horizon. Every week the *Athenaeum* reviewed, briefly, three to six books of new verse. Almost all of them were bad, though the reviewer displayed no ability to distinguish among them. In an article written in 1913 Norman Douglas describes the authors of these numerous volumes as 'Children who have ceased growing in mind and who, for all their variety, have one dominant characteristic: that love of laying bare certain private little affairs of their own which looks uncommonly like a spiritualized form of exhibitionism'.[44]

Some titles from the *Athenaeum*'s short reviews during January and February 1913, together with one or two phrases of the criticism, evoke the pervading literary atmosphere of the time:

> *Songs of God and Man*—Anna Bunston
> ('freshness and spirituality')
> *Songs of Sunlight: Verses from Many Lands*—Rev. Sir George Ralph Fetherston
> ('nobility of sentiment')
> *Dainty Verses for Little Folk*—Augusta Hancock
> ('written in the right spirit')
> *The Chief Incidents of the 'Titanic' Wreck*, treated in Verse— Edwin Drew
> ('may appeal to those who lost friends in this appalling catastrophe')
> *Judith, and Other Poems*—H.L.
> ('lacks for the most part the true poet's inspiration . . . one or two touches, however')
> *Some Adventures of the Soul and the Deliverer*— C. M. Verschoyle
> ('mystical and religious tendency, not without merit')
> *Idylls of the East*—Edward Bennett
> ('a pleasing note of sincerity)'

Among these 'reviews' one finds also

> *Love Poems and Others*—D. H. Lawrence
> ('an exalted and impressive imagery is mixed with metaphors that closely approach bathos')
> *A Boy's Will*—Robert Frost
> ('many of his verses do not rise above the ordinary, though here and there a happy line or phrase lingers gratefully in the memory')

In these conditions it is not surprising that it was still possible for a book of verse—if its defects were of the kind which pleased the influential publishers and reviewers of the day—to become quite suddenly a 'best-seller'. In its issue of 20 June 1914 the *Athenaeum*'s column 'Literary Gossip' declared:

'Mr John Oxenham published a small book of poems *Bees in Amber*, last September through Messrs Chatto & Windus. It is already in a fourteenth edition, a fact which should encourage the aspiring poet of today. The public is not so blind to merit as it is sometimes thought to be.'

If any 'aspiring poet' of the day went in search of such encouragement, he discovered nothing new. There is an Author's Apology in which Oxenham explains that the inspirations which arrive to interrupt other 'more profitable work' are like bees in his bonnet which he must pluck out and set in the amber of verse— hence the title. And there are the 'bees' themselves, whose sweetness no Georgian could hope to rival.

Another 'best-selling' poet of these years was Patrick MacGill. His first book, published when the author was nineteen, sold 8,000 copies; his second[45] exceeded this number. Again the quality of the verses ('dedicated to my pick and shovel') suggests a low level of public taste:

> 'He is the drainer—
>   Out on the moorland bleak and grey,
> using his spade in a primitive way, through
> chilly evening and searing day. Call him a
> fool and well you may—
>   He is the drainer.'

Yet in the face of all this the *Athenaeum* could still look forward gladly to the final vulgarization of literature:

'The only poetry which can save us is a poetry of the people, for the people, and, in the end, by the people; if you will, a poetry which is gloriously and unashamedly "vulgar" . . . Poetry and art must be born again, and born like every saviour of mankind, in humility among labouring people.'[46]

No new poetry of substance could be written by men who remained dependent on the approval of popular reviewers and the general public at this time. There were no means by which good new poetry could find a wide audience. In these circumstances the young poets of real talent could only write what would flout public taste, and hope that in time readers would come to judge them fairly. The Georgians were not reactionary writers: in many ways they were daringly new. But in such a situation they were not daring enough. In this matter of the relation between poet and audience, a more violent thrust than theirs was required if a correct distance was to be achieved.

REFERENCES

1. Introduction to *Literary Essays of Ezra Pound*, 1954.
2. 'Homage to Sextus Propertius' XII.
3. *Books and Persons*, pp. 88, 89.
4. *Return to Yesterday* (Reminiscences 1894–1914), p. 181.
5. *Books and Persons*, p. 92.
6. *Return to Yesterday*, pp. 377 and 492.
7. *Books and Persons*, p. 204.
8. 'The Artist and the Public', *English Review*, October 1913.
9. *Personae* (Collected Shorter Poems), p. 203.
10. *Books and Persons*, p. 92.
11. See *Literary Essays of Ezra Pound*, Faber 1954, p. 81.
12. *The Poetry of Ezra Pound*, Hugh Kenner, Appendix I, p. 308.
13. *The Later Life and Letters of Sir Henry Newbolt*, p. 106.
14. *The Criterion*, July 1932. cf. Pound, Canto LXXX.
15. *The Later Life and Letters of Sir Henry Newbolt*, pp. 8, 9.
16. *The Sacred Wood*, 1960 edition, p. 24.
17. *The Later Life and Letters of Sir Henry Newbolt*, p. 9.
18. *Essays* (1924), p. 240.
19. *Literary Essays of Ezra Pound*, 1954, p. 81.
20. Op. cit., p. 229.
21. *Ezra Pound* (Essays on Pound edited by Peter Russell), p. 260.
22. *Return to Yesterday*, p. 45.
23. ibid., p. 85.
24. *Books and Persons*, p. 125.
25. 23 July 1909.
26. 18 November 1909.
27. 20 May 1909.
28. *The Letters of Ezra Pound*, p. 42.
29. ibid.
30. *Eddie Marsh: Sketches Compiled by Christopher Hassall and Dennis Matthews*, p. 25.
31. *Georgian Poetry, 1911–1912*.
32. *The Later Life and Letters of Sir Henry Newbolt*, p. 207.
33. ibid., p. 314.

34. Pound, *Letters*, p. 48.

35. F. S. Flint. *The Criterion*, July 1932. The 'votary' was Hewlett, not Beerbohm.

36. ibid.

37. *Poetry and Drama*, June 1913, p. 126.

38. ibid., p. 135.

39. ibid., September 1913, p. 271.

40. ibid., March 1914, p. 52.

41. Quoted in *Poetry and Drama*, September 1913.

42. Reported in *Poetry and Drama*, June 1914, p. 122.

43. *Pencraft: A Plea for Older Ways*, p. 50. 'Singer' in the critical language of the time must be read as 'poet'.

44. 'Modern Minstrelsy', the *English Review*, January 1913.

45. *Songs of the Dead End*, the Yearbook Press, 1912.

46. 'The Great Schism', June 1917.

4

1909–16: 'POETRY' versus 'LIFE'

Imperialists; Georgians; War poets

'Ah! It's a Great Age to live in—the high dawn of
England. . . . Think of the fleet going up the Dardanelles.
Think of the Centuries—think of Chivalry victorious.'
HENRY NEWBOLT
(from a letter written during the First World War)

'. . . the true Poets must be truthful.'
WILFRED OWEN

THE relation between the widely known poetry of 1909 and the
great events of the day is not a subtle one. Events stimulated the
poets to write poetry in the established manner; the poet openly
committed his work to one or another point of view in public
matters in a way which sacrificed depth to readily grasped
generalities. Before discussing the qualities of this poetry it will
be helpful to look back briefly to the time which established
Rudyard Kipling, William Watson, Henry Newbolt, and Alfreds
Austin and Noyes as the men from whom the general reading
public of 1909 expected to receive its poetry.

Although Kipling, Henley, Watson, and Austin were all writing
during the 1890s, the decade is generally thought of as belonging
to the 'Aesthetes'. This is because Wilde and his associates, though
they scorned the public, were not ignored by it. Recalling the
period of the *Yellow Book* F. M. Ford writes:

'The Book World was electric. Books were everywhere.
Accounts of the personal habits of writers filled the daily papers.

67

Minute volumes of poems in limited editions fetched unheard of prices at auctions. It was good to be a writer in England. And it is to be remembered that as far as that particular body [the Aesthetes] were concerned the rewards were earned. They were skilful and earnest writers. They were an immense improvement on their predecessors. They were genuine men of letters. . . .

'But all that went with the trial of Wilde. . . .

'Wilde then brought down the *Yellow Book* group and most of the other lyrists of London that for its year or two had been a nest of singing birds.'[a]

One is helped towards an explanation of the public's willingness (before the collapse described above) at least to acknowledge Oscar Wilde's status as a writer in his own lifetime by some remarks of Mr A. E. Rodway:

'After all "decadence" can be regarded as "a form of imperialism of the spirit, ambitious, arrogant, aggressive, waving the flag of human power over an ever wider and wider territory". Indeed, Wilde really expresses the self-confident expansiveness of a secure age much more than Kipling does, who often reminds one of a man cheering to keep his courage up.'[2]

In one respect the 'aesthetic' pose of writers like Wilde—their insistence that all art was 'useless', that it bore no direct relation to 'life'—can be seen as an attitude deliberately taken up in a particular political and social context. The rejection of politics from art was itself a political action: the aesthetic doctrine was for Wilde (as, Professor L. C. Knights points out, the aristocratic banner was for Yeats[3]) 'his red flag, something with which to make offensive gestures'; or, in the words of Mr A. E. Rodway, 'a red rag to John Bull, who believed in Wordsworth, Tennyson, and Art-for-Morality's sake'.[4]

The public's sudden and violent rejection of the Aesthetes, and its wholehearted turning to the 'healthy' school of patriot poets was more than anything a reflection of political change. Victorianism had begun to decline:

[a] The first paragraph of this quotation is confirmed by an article which appeared in *The Yellow Book*, January 1895, by Max Beerbohm.

'The death of Gordon had lowered British prestige in the East; at home, the influx of American prairie wheat was increasing agricultural distress; in the United States, production was increasing faster than in England; the Home Rule problem was becoming more acute, German competition more successful; and working class unrest, as the Dock Strike of 1899 showed, was taking an organized form. The solid Victorian age was coming to an end. . . .'[5]

As this ending began to be generally felt the forces of conservatism asserted themselves. And in the literary sphere they found a solid reason in the trial of Wilde, for throwing out the aesthetic movement as a whole. The political pendulum, F. M. Ford recalls, swung violently towards the right:

'The artistic activities of the physical force schools of Henley or of Mr Rudyard Kipling were to find, in the world, their counterparts in outrages—wars, rumours of wars, pogroms, repressions.'[6]

By 1906 the Conservatives had been beaten in a General Election by the combined Liberal and Labour Parties; but in literature—essentially a concern of the middle class—conservatism asserted itself even more strongly. The liberal tendencies of a small group of intellectuals and writers received little support from established journals and publishers, and it was not until the appearance of the Georgians that the new liberal movement found its way successfully into poetry.

Thus the poetry we find established in 1909 is a poetry of political retrenchment, committed to conserve political and social ideas and institutions doomed to collapse. Like all intellectual rearguard actions this one can afford to give nothing away, and is forced more and more to treat complex problems as though their solutions were simple to all but the dull-witted. In their own defence against what little remains of the aesthetic movement these poets assert that their work springs from direct contact with 'life', and that this is something they share with all great poets. 'Life is their object,' Newbolt wrote of the literary public, 'and art is not their life. . . .'

'If, then, they come to the artist it is for something that will help them to the fuller life, and they demand of him not merely that he shall excel in expression, but that he shall excellently express feelings such as they can understand and value. They demand that he shall chant to them, for example, their own morality, their own religion, their own patriotism.'[7]

Newbolt and Kipling, in particular, experienced as poets that close involvement with political movements into which Yeats allowed himself to emerge only with the caution described in chapter two. For the sake of 'perfection of the work' Yeats was always prepared to disappoint the Irish patriots. 'Perfection' was no object of Kipling or Newbolt, and English patriotism was never disappointed by them. For this reason they enjoyed at times a political importance which was mistaken for a literary one. Newbolt, for example, describes[8] how verses of his influenced an election (to the delight of Kipling), and concludes his account of the occasion with a quotation from G. M. Trevelyan:

'Such, in those days, was the close connection of poetry and politics, when poetry could serve the purpose of pamphleteering.'

Looking back on his life as a writer Newbolt expresses a delight in his own successes. In the present age it is difficult to take the following quotation seriously; but in the literary discourse of pre-1914 England this was unquestionably one kind of success:

'I've had in the last twenty years all the satisfaction that could ever be got out of the place—I've written and published in *The Times*, or on public monuments, all the Trafalgar Odes and commemorative verses that were wanted. "What asketh a man to have?" . . .
'What fun we've had!
'Even now they're asking me for an inscription for the great monument on Helles Point in Gallipoli—the monument to which all nations dip their flags in passing.'[9]

The illusion collectively held by these men was that they wrote about 'life', that they were in touch with reality. In fact most of their poems had as little relevance to ordinary living as the poems of the 'nineties; but they were more damaging to literature because of the great claims made for them. The poet is once again established as a 'philosopher'.

An article in the *Quarterly Review* on the Poet Laureate[10] exemplifies the approach to poetry re-established after the collapse of the aesthetic movement. The writer begins by making a simple distinction between 'subjective or lyrical' poets (with Sappho and Keats as examples) and 'objective' poetry (examples: Dante, Shakespeare, and Goethe). The 'primary requisite' of the first kind is 'a peculiar personal sensitiveness or passion'; but for poetry of the objective kind the primary equipment of the poet must include much more than this:

'It must include a wide outlook on life, an instinctive insight into the motives of other men and women and the varieties of human circumstance, together with some formal or at all events some virtual philosophy, by which the facts of life are bound together or focalized ... In other words when we are dealing with any objective poet—and the greatest poets of the world have belonged to this order—*the ultimate standard by which his rank and his significance are to be measured is what he means as a thinker*, as an observer, as an impassioned critic of life, not the manner in which he produces his notes as a singer. The importance of the latter is vital, but is subsidiary to the importance of the former.'[11]

There is in this statement the primary division—between meaning and expression, or content and form—which has haunted English poetry for more than a hundred years, the emphasis passing from one to the other always unsatisfactorily. More must be said about this problem later. It is enough for the moment to point to the great dangers in the attitude expressed, an attitude widely held in 1909. For poetry with an apparently abstractable 'content' which coincided with general feelings was declared to be philosophically sound; while that which seemed to run against, or to ignore, popular opinion, was declared to be unsound. In the article here referred to, Alfred Austin is treated as an 'objective poet', and a great one, though it is admitted that his style is not particularly good! Further, the critic finds the

cause of Austin's philosophical and moral profundity in his
national consciousness. He is, admittedly, a Roman Catholic.
But 'whatever might be the influence of dogma or faith upon
his nature' he is nevertheless 'not an abstract man but a concrete
individual Englishman who, no matter what his religion, [con-
fronts] this world *and the next* as a member of the great race. . . .'[a]

Having established Austin's 'philosophy' in a healthy context
the critic proceeds to describe it:

'For Mr Austin love of country is closely associated with a
philosophy of social life which is, in an age like the present, so
distinct and challenging as to merit the appellation of polemical.'

But when this 'challenging' philosophy is outlined it is seen to
be nothing more than the sentimental conservatism of an
idealized Old England which reasserted itself strongly in the first
years of this century:

'Every rank and avocation, from the peasant's up to the
prince's, has, in his view, its proper dignity, and, when set in
appropriate circumstances, its proper beauty. Wealth, as he conceives it, is ideally the symbolical ornament and the necessary
material mechanism of certain high activities, far-reaching social
services, and lives whose wholesome tenor becomes influential
by reason of their conspicuous stateliness. . . .'

The writer now forgets his adjectives 'distinct' and 'challenging',
and continues:

'There is nothing original in such a philosophy of life, and
herein lies one of Mr Austin's characteristic merits. . . . It is
essentially the poetry of commonsense and healthy directness.'

After further insistence that 'Mr Austin's criticisms of life . . . do
not differ from those of any more sober censor, except for the

---

a Italics mine. If this consciousness of oneself as 'a member of the
great race' carried weight in heaven, it was surely important in assessing
the worth of a man's poetry!

flights of exaggeration with which his poetic genius invests them', the critic goes on:

'We are not however insisting on Mr Austin's want of moral originality as a defect. We should, indeed, do better to call it his want of moral eccentricity. . . . [His poems] exhibit before all things a normal and healthy man, in close contact with realities. . . . He is not a poet as distinguished from a man of the world, but he is a man of the world distinguished by possessing the temperament of a poet.'

Here then we have a sketch of what it was to be a great poet in 1909: a man who expressed a sound philosophy in verse. And a sound philosophy was, in the reigning literary circles of the time, a philosophy of irrational conservatism. The poet is 'a man of the world', 'a normal and healthy man in close contact with realities', with 'a practical attitude of mind and a closeness to common life'. He is a good chap, and certainly not an artist, for the word artist bore 'associations with foreigners and long-haired aesthetes', and was out of favour.[12]

One poem[13] of Alfred Austin's will serve to illustrate this healthy 'want of moral eccentricity' in the face of the political and social uncertainties which could throw up on the one hand Bernard Shaw and on the other Oscar Wilde:

Why England is Conservative

I

Because of our dear Mother, the fair Past,
On whom twin Hope and Memory safely lean,
And from whose fostering wisdom none shall wean
Their love and faith, while love and faith shall last:
Mother of happy homes and Empire vast,
Of hamlets meek, and many a proud demesne,
Blue spires of cottage smoke 'mong woodlands green,
And comely altars where no stone is cast.
And shall we barter these for gaping Throne,
Dismantled towers, mean plots without a tree,
A herd of hinds too equal to be free,

Greedy of other's, jealous of their own,
And, where sweet Order now breathes cadenced tone,
Envy, and hate, and all uncharity?

II

Banish that fear! 'Twere infamy to yield
To folly what to force had been denied,
Or in the Senate quail before the tide
We should have stemmed and routed in the field.

This is social reaction in the guise of poetry, working to under-mine the efforts of men who were attempting to face honestly the problems of the day. The writer's concern is not literary but political—an unbalance at least as serious to literature as the unbalance of the Aesthetes. The highly developed sense of fact which T. S. Eliot writes of as an essential element in the produc-tion of poetry is totally absent. The 'happy homes', 'hamlets meek', 'proud demesnes' and 'Blue spires of cottage smoke 'mong woodlands green' sentimentalize and generalize for the sake of a public cause outside the poem; while the alternatives to the *status quo* are distorted in images of chaos and decay: 'gaping Throne', 'dismantled towers', and 'plots without a tree'. Finally the new social ideas are routed by a suggestion that they are foreign—the implication that being so they are inferior, needing no special emphasis:

'Domain, Throne, Altar still may be upheld,
So we disdain, as we disdained of yore,
The foreign froth that foams against our shore,
Only by its white cliffs to be repelled!'

The third section then returns to an idealized, unchanging England, in lines which, unrelated to their time, would be a pleasant ineffectual exercise in the use of a dead language; but which, in the face of the realities of poverty and injustice, repre-sent a dishonesty immoral in its effect as no poem of the Aesthetes ever was, for the poem poses and is accepted as the wisdom of 'a man of the world and a philosopher':

'Therefore, chime sweet and safely, village bells,
And, rustic chancels, woo to reverent prayer,
And wise and simple to the porch repair
Round which Death, slumbering, dreamlike heaves and swells.
Let hound and horn in wintry woods and dells
Make jocund music though the boughs be bare,
And whistling yokel guide his teaming share
Hard by the homes where gentle lordship dwells.
Therefore sit high enthroned on every hill,
Authority! and loved in every vale;
Nor, old Tradition, falter in the tale
Of lowly valour led by lofty will:
And, though the throats of envy rage and rail,
Be fair proud England, proud fair England still!'

Kipling is, of course, the most popular and the most widely read of the 'public' poets who dominated the poetic scene after the turn of the century. He is a writer of much greater skill and energy than the more 'refined' poets who shared with him the attentions of the literary public; and reputable critics have treated him as an important writer. A full assessment of Kipling's poetry is not relevant to this essay. What is important is to insist that where he used his poetry to meet social and political problems— that is, whenever his poetry is 'public'—he does not come to terms with the complexity of his subject as I have suggested Yeats does in 'Easter 1916'; instead, he simplifies, and clouds the deficiencies of his position in rhetoric.

As Professor Pinto has said, 'he surrendered himself completely to the vulgar ethics of the crowd'.

'Like the typical "man of action" of his period, he loved facts but hated and feared reality. All his work is coloured by his denial of the existence of the fundamental problems of the modern world. There was no Irish or South African problem, only rebels and traitors; there was no aesthetic problem, only wasters and rotters like Sir Anthony Gloster's son who was educated at "Harrer an' Trinity College" and "muddled with books and pictures", and Tomlinson whose sins were entirely literary; there was no problem of war and peace, only foolish liberals and sentimental or knavish pacifists. All the world needed was more discipline, obedience and loyalty, and above all a paternal British Empire with its unselfish and efficient administrators and admirable army licked into shape by perfect N.C.O.s.'[14]

Further, whatever reasons may be advanced for treating Kipling's poetry as literature, it is clear that its quality as literature had nothing to do with its popularity. The reading public of 1909 was not inclined to treat poetry 'as poetry, and not another thing'. It was the 'other thing' that mattered (as Kipling knew); poetry was only another vehicle on which opinion and prejudice could be trundled into the drawing-room. '[Kipling's] vogue among the hordes of the respectable', Arnold Bennett wrote in 1909,

'was due to political reasons, and . . . he retains his authority over the said hordes because he is the bard of their prejudices and their clayey ideals. *A democrat with ten times Kipling's gift and power could never have charmed and held the governing classes as Kipling has done.*'[15]

Henry Newbolt made himself popular in the same way, but perhaps at a different social level. His audience was probably a stratum above Kipling's—the upper middle class—and consequently smaller. Newbolt was a more liberal imperialist, more tolerant of education and art, more reasonable generally. But again his prestige depended on the opinions he versified, and his poems simplified complex problems. Cricket, boxing, and soldiering were all part of the same healthy public school game for Newbolt:

> 'To set the cause above renown,
>   To love the game beyond the prize,
> To honour while you strike him down,
>   The foe that comes with fearless eyes;
> To count the life of battle good,
>   And dear the land that gave you birth,
> And dearer yet the brotherhood
>   That binds the brave of all the earth.'[16]

The facts of war as it had been in the past and was again to be in 1914 are lost in the haze of an imprecise emotion. Newbolt records in some diary notes:

'I spent most of the years of my life under the certainty of war, the conviction that my country must pass through the trial of a great war; the necessary efforts of training for it the force and the thoughts and the character.'[17]

Yet like all the poets of the time who claimed to be 'close to life' in their work, his conception of this struggle was quite unreal. It is embodied, for example, in the poem 'Vitai Lampada', in which the schoolboy hero graduates from cricket to soldiering:

'The sand of the desert is sodden red,—
   Red with the wreck of a square that broke;—
The Gatling's jammed and the Colonel's dead,
   And the regiment blind with dust and smoke.
The river of death has brimmed its banks,
   And England's far, and Honour a name,
But the voice of a schoolboy rallies the ranks:
   "Play up! play up! and play the game!" '

The unreality of this is evident before the irrelevance and absurdity of the final line is reached. Death and blood are a harmless convention in these poems, as they are in Western films. They bear no relation to blood that pulses from a severed artery, nor betray any of that sense of the appalling finality of death in war discovered, for example, in the letters and poems of Wilfred Owen. His concern is to 'keep the Nelson touch',[18] not to come to terms with things as they are. And with this aim, he echoes the same irrational conservatism that made Austin and Kipling popular:

'Then let Memory tell thy heart;
 "England! what thou wert, thou art!"
 Gird thee with thine ancient might
 Forth! and God defend the Right!'[19]

   The crude division between 'meaning' and 'form'—or, in the reviewer's jargon of the time, between the poet's 'message' and the poet's 'song'—remained a staple in the criticism of poetry up to the time of the war. The aesthetic half of the argument continued to find supporters after 1900 (notably Yeats), but its opponents by 1909 were more numerous, more widely published, and more generally respected. In various ways the old argument continued to be brought into the discussion of poetry, almost always with the intention of supporting the public moralist against the private aesthete:

'It is only public events which will arouse Mr Watson to anything like passion, and in this more than anything else he resembles the poets of an old, of an almost vanished school. In a world where poetry has become a vehicle only for intimate self-revelations, Mr Watson remains calmly impersonal. He wears the cloak of the grand manner in an age of little men and we hope when he ascends—surely the last poet to enter Parnassus—his place may not be very far from the tranquil throne of Wordsworth.'[20]

This rubbing of salt into the wounds of aestheticism was of course unnecessary. The 'cloak of the grand manner' was worn by all the widely known poets of the day except Yeats; their work, if it was to remain popular, could not be 'difficult or introspective'.[21] But for the sake of good health the lesson that 'ideas' were more important than 'art' (a word still out of favour) was continually preached:

'If there is one great need in the literature of today [Alfred Noyes wrote[22]] it is that we should regain the power of co-ordinating the whole world of ideas. We shall never again have a great world-poetry so long as we merely specialize in pessimism, in optimism, in imperialism, in Celticism.'

What poetry wants, he says, is 'the cosmic sweep'; and he warns significantly

'There is a tendency to be too deliberately artistic—a transitional stage between that of the mere Philistine and that of the artist to whom the method of expression has become so natural that he thinks no more about it. But, indeed, something of the Philistine, something of his great stupid superiority to mere tricks and turns of phrasing, is found in the simplicity of all great art.'

The lesson is repeated in the same journal by Holbrook Jackson.[23] The result which follows when the artist permits himself 'to be driven from the broad paths of life into those narrow grooves where he may receive the appreciation and rewards of only cultured and refined people' is that his art becomes 'exotic, foreign to the average taste'.

'Only the upholders of the narrow and limited view of art, the minor artists and their supporters, desire to limit art entirely to the self-expression of a special and often rather feverish type of being; the nervous, over-strung and egotistical type, that we call artist today.'

Against these writers' insistence that poetry ought to be 'dependent on the average man'[24] the ghost of aestheticism occasionally raised its wrong-but-more-reasonable voice. J. M. Robertson, for example,[25] criticized the moralist poets, taking William Watson as one of his examples:

'Seldom, perhaps, has he had a larger measure of political sympathy than when he championed the causes of Armenia and Greece against the late Sultan Abdul. . . . But the judgment conveyed its own confutation. . . . Mr. Watson's philosophy, we feel, is here after all a philosophy of rhetoric, making the old play with the worshipped Name, staking all on the afflatus of the tripod, solving the riddle of the painful earth by the science of the chivalrous schoolboy. . . . To our generation, stirred by the sense of wrong inwoven in the fabric of all things national, Mr Watson's political psalmody is hardly more impressive than that of Tennyson in the last generation, when the tripodic vocabulary was sounded on the side of the very Turkey of Mr Watson's damnation. We can only question, as did Hobbes between Milton and Salmasius, whose style is the finer and whose politics is worse.
'It is the old fatality. The poet bent on great things must needs sing moral truth, and inspire right action: it is his congenital burden so to yearn; and yet in the nature of things he cannot so fulfil himself and still be a poet.'

In this, Robertson comes closer to a full realization of the dilemma of modern English poetry than any of the writers of the

time so far quoted in this chapter. And in his specific criticisms
of poets, Robertson is sound. Pointing out that Alfred Noyes
offers 'dogma, vociferation, sermonizing' instead of poetry, he
goes on:

'To set out at this time of day in a planned epic to solemnize
the story of Drake and to heat the ashes of England's ancient
quarrel with Spain is to cater for schoolboys. . . . His purpose,
on any view, is insularly didactic, and his execution responds to
his flawed intention.'

Yet when Robertson comes to suggest a solution to the dilemma
he can only fall back on what he calls 'the truth underlying the
often misconceived doctrine of "Art for Art's Sake".' One can
accept the first half of his argument: that the poet is no teacher.
But the second half is inadequate; it sees the poet as

'the harp of the winds of feeling, an exquisite word instrument to
give cadence and charm to any or all the passions of men.'

We have already observed that Yeats, by coming to terms with
the complexity of events, was to achieve more than Robertson
here considers possible. And T. S. Eliot, while leaning in his
early work towards aesthetic principles in order to avoid the
moralist position, also constructed his own path out of the
sterility of 'Art for Art's Sake'.

The struggle between 'Art' and 'Life' in English poetry took a
new turn with the appearance of the Georgian anthologies. I
have already indicated (in Chapter 3) that the changes in literary
fashion which took place during the 1920's have obscured the
critical view of the Georgians in relation to their time. Mr David
Daiches' comments on them[26] are typical:

'There are two main reasons which compel men to combine
into armies—attack and defence. If . . . the Georgians were
not making an attack, the possibility suggests itself that their
common purpose was one of defence. And this seems to be
the truth of the matter. If we scan the body of poetry published in these volumes and endeavour to see its place in the

development of post-Victorian literature, it is not difficult to realise that the common aim of the Georgian poets was retrenchment.'

I have no wish to present any one of the Georgians as a great poet, nor to suggest that as a group they made profound discoveries in the writing of poetry. But it is important to see them clearly historically. Mr Daiches has not seen the place of the Georgian movement 'in the development of post-Victorian literature'; if he had he would not have suggested that theirs was a poetry of retrenchment. The reviewer of the first anthology who described it as the vehicle of 'the new rebellion' presumably found in it new tendencies which threatened the real poetry of retrenchment—that of the poets already discussed in this chapter. Mr Daiches, like so many critics of the past twenty years, has seen the Georgians through spectacles provided for him by the later, more vigorous movement led by Pound and Eliot. The suggestion is that the Georgians set themselves against the natural development of modern poetry: in fact they were its precursors. It is therefore worth examining some Georgian poetry in order to illustrate in what ways it represented a revolt against the established poetry of the time.

In the course of his *Quarterly Review* notice[27] Arthur Waugh tries to explain why he considers the Georgians lack 'beauty and spirituality':

'Life it [their poetry] has in abundance, the fierce feverish life of a mind that has not yet established its relations with its environment, and is perpetually launching excursions into new territory, without consolidating the ground that it has won. It is the life, in fact, of experiments and moods; and the poetry in which it issues is precisely that poetry of the mood and of the emotion, which we have defined as lacking in the sound foundations and universal significance of the poetry of ideas. The general atmosphere is that of a world in which there is no prevailing current of ideas, no pervading intellectual stimulus, and from which the natural refuge is found in the exaggeration of trivial incidents into some sort of symbolic relationship with big movements, and in the acceptance of individual whims and wayward fancies in the place of firm philosophical ideals.'

A fair criticism of the Georgians could have been made on these lines; but Waugh was not the man to make it. Belonging to the school of critics who read poetry for the 'ideas' it expressed, judging it good if the ideas corresponded with their own, he was bewildered by a poetry which refused to move from specific location and specific incident into generalization.

The real achievement of the Georgians was in the attempt to confine poetry within the limits of what had actually been experienced. It is a negative achievement perhaps, but it resulted in poems rather than the versified argument which would have pleased the *Quarterly Review*. And it was precisely this honesty and directness of approach that Arthur Waugh found bewildering. Describing the group characteristics he had noticed, Waugh commented:

' "We write nothing that we might not speak" proclaims the new rebellion in effect: "We draw the thing as we see it for the God of things as they are. Every aspect of life shall be the subject of our art, and what we see we shall describe in the language we use every day." '

Waugh's objection to this is that life as experienced is not 'philosophic'; that 'things as they are' are not 'beautiful'; and that ordinary language is not 'poetic'.

In the work of the Georgians 'poetry' and 'life' begin to merge again: art is not for them something fragile, magical, and remote from ordinary living, as it was for the aesthetes; nor is life equated with politics, public affairs, and large conservative generalizations as it was for the imperialists. Life for them was what they experienced. Brooke unwittingly speaks for the group when he describes, in a letter to a friend, his constant habit of mind:

'It consists in just looking at people and things as themselves —neither as useful nor moral nor ugly nor anything else; but just as being.'[28]

This was a safe starting point, if it could be achieved, for it meant that the poet could observe, free from the mists of prejudice which clouded the vision of men like Kipling. Brooke's poetry is trivial because much of his life is trivial—limited by certain habits of mind learned in a public school, and cushioned from large areas of uncomfortable fact by unearned income. But one feels in his writings an impulse which was driving him in the direction that a poet of his time needed to take. And in taking this direction he met with opposition:

'. . . it's really been rather a shock to me [he writes in one of his letters]—and made me momentarily hopeless—that so many intelligent and well-tasted people didn't seem to have any idea of what I was driving at, in any poem of the last few years. It opened my eyes to the fact that people who like poetry are barely more common than people who like pictures.'[29]

As well as the attacks of the 'ideas' school represented by the *Quarterly Review*, Brooke suffered the more direct personal expressions of puzzlement from the dilettanti of letters:

'Mrs Cornford tried to engage me in a controversy over the book—she and her school. They are known as the Heart-criers, because they believe all poetry should be short, simple, naive, and a cry from the heart; the sort of thing an inspired child might write if it was in the habit of posing to its elders. They object to my poetry as unreal, affected, complex, "literary", and full of long words.'[30]

This letter puts Brooke's poetry in its historical context. To many, he appeared an intellectual poet, because more agility of mind was required in a poem which attempted to come to terms with the complexity of specific events or situations than in poetry which versified ready-made ideas or 'poetic' sentiments. It is not surprising, then, to find Henry Newbolt writing of Brooke:

'He is gifted with an intellectual curiosity and a natural and habitual intensity of feeling that recall the work of Donne and of Donne only among the English poets.'[31]

But irrespective of the kind of response his poetry received, Brooke felt the limitations of what he was writing, and moved slowly towards something better. When his publisher asked him to remove one of his notorious 'unpleasant' poems, he wrote:

'My own feeling is that to remove it would be to overbalance the book still more in the direction of unimportant prettiness. There's plenty of that sort of wash in the other pages for readers who like it. . . . About a lot of the book I occasionally feel that like Ophelia I've turned "Thought and affliction, passion, hell itself, to favour and to prettiness".'[32]

There is of course no point in attempting to prove that he would have become a considerable poet had he lived. The point is simply that Brooke, a representative Georgian, was moving in a direction which was advantageous to the development of English poetry. He helped to prepare the ground for the work of better poets. Even in 'Grantchester'—the poem which critics wishing to minimize the importance of the Georgians understandably select for discussion—Brooke is ashamed enough of its Newboltesque couplet,

> 'For England's the one land, I know,
> Where men with Splendid Hearts may go,'

to spend the twenty-four lines which follow it demonstrating clumsily that it is only meant as a joke.

When the war came Brooke departed from the manner most characteristic of the Georgians and wrote the sonnets by which he is best known—

'Now God be thanked Who has matched us with His hour' etc.

He died before experiencing any of the real horror of war; and it was left to other members of the group to bring what might be called their 'technique of honesty' to fulfilment in poems which faced the reality of that horror.

I have suggested that the imperialist poets were prevented from telling the truth by their commitment to conserve all they could out of the general decay of Victorianism. The Georgians on the other hand—even in the name they chose for themselves—asserted freedom from Victorian ideas; and the younger writers used this freedom best. Wilfred Wilson Gibson's poem 'Geraniums' in the first Anthology is an example of the kind of experience which poets committed on the one hand to 'beauty' and on the other to the presentation of England as 'Mother of happy homes and Empire vast', chose to keep out of their poetry:

'Stuck in a bottle on the window-sill,
In the cold gaslight burning gaily red
Against the luminous blue of London night,
These flowers are mine: while somewhere out of sight
In some black-throated alley's stench and heat,
Oblivious of the racket of the street,
A poor old weary woman lies in bed.

'Broken with lust and drink, blear-eyed and ill,
Her battered bonnet nodding on her head,
From a dark arch she clutched my sleeve and said:
"I've sold no bunch today, nor touched a bite . . .
Son, buy six-pennorth; and 't will mean a bed."

'So blazing gaily red
Against the luminous deeps
Of starless London night,
They burn for my delight:
While somewhere, snug in bed,
A worn old woman sleeps.

'And yet tomorrow will these blooms be dead
With all their lively beauty; and tomorrow
May end the light lusts and the heavy sorrow
Of that old body with the nodding head.
The last oath muttered, the last pint drained deep,
She'll sink, as Cleopatra sank, to sleep;
Nor need to barter blossoms for a bed.'[33]

The Georgians belonged to the new liberal intellectual group that grew steadily in numbers during the first decade of this century; and their type is perhaps best illustrated by the Schlegel sisters in E. M. Forster's novel *Howards End*. They did not consider it bad taste (as the Wilcox type did in the same novel) to discuss social problems. They were willing to think of the Leonard Basts and the geranium sellers of the world as human beings worthy of consideration. Politically they were 'affiliated with the then dominant Liberal party';[34] intellectually they asserted 'that this new Georgian age should begin clear of all the muddled notions of its amorphous predecessor'.[35] The Wilcox type on the other hand were imperialists of the Tory, rather than of the new 'liberal imperialist' kind, and undoubtedly approved of Henry Newbolt's Trafalgar Day odes in *The Times*.

Yet the Georgians were limited in their experience, and confused in their attitude to the public. The movement was firm in its denial of 'all formally religious, philosophic or improving themes; and all sad, wicked, café table themes';[36] but as Robert Graves points out, this resulted most often 'in a poetry which could be praised rather for what it was not than for what it was'.[37] The weakness of their position is essentially the weakness of the Schlegels' position in *Howards End*; and the passage in which Helen Schlegel looks out over the landscape and asks herself who is the real inheritor of England might be taken as representative of the Georgian dilemma:

'Does [England] belong to those who have moulded her and made her feared by other lands, or to those who have added nothing to her power, but have somehow seen her, seen the whole island at once, lying as a jewel in a silver sea, sailing as a ship of souls, with all the brave world's fleet accompanying her towards eternity?'

—a sentence which has something of the honesty of the Georgians and something of the unpleasant softness of their lyricism at its worst.

Writing about contemporary poetry in 1917,[38] T. S. Eliot made two important points. First, a general point, that

'One of the ways by which contemporary verse has tried to escape the rhetorical, the abstract, the moralizing, to recover (for that is its purpose) the accents of direct speech, is to concentrate its attention on trivial or accidental or commonplace objects.'

And second, writing specifically of the Georgians,

'. . . it is not unworthy to notice how often the word "little" occurs; and how this word is used, not merely as a piece of information, but with a caress, a conscious delight.'

These two comments placed together are important; they explain one another and throw light on the limitations and the achievements of Georgian poetry. The impossibility of separating poetic technique and social intention is again demonstrated. Just as Eliot himself (and other poets of the 1920's), concerned with achieving firmness of outline and discipline of emotion, unconsciously inserted the words 'dry' and 'hard', or images of deserts, rocks and bones, into poetry; so the Georgians, repudiating what they considered to be the large, sweeping dishonesties of their immediate predecessors, unconsciously reduced their subjects to honest proportions by an insistence on 'littleness'. The dominant images of three decades of poetry, even when they spring initially from a literary concern, carry accurately the mood, and in a sense the history, of England during that time: Drake and Nelson; rural England;[a] fear in a handful of dust. The Georgians realized the total inadequacy of the mode of thought which saw England in terms of Drake and Nelson. They believed they had escaped from that dishonesty, and D. H. Lawrence was right when he found in *Georgian Poetry 1911–1912* 'a big breath taken when we are waking up after a night of repressive dreams', an immense joy in the direct experience of life concretely embodied in landscape, free from abstract thought and rhetoric.[39] The awakening came too late, however, and among the young who had no power to alter events. War came, and the honesty of the new poets was turned towards 'war, and the pity of war'; the poetry was now in the pity, no longer in the joy:

> 'When lo! an angel called him out of heaven,
> Saying, Lay not thy hand upon the lad,
> Neither do anything to him. Behold,
> A ram, caught in a thicket by its horns;
> Offer the Ram of Pride instead of him.
> But the old man would not so, but slew his son,—
> And half of the seed of Europe, one by one.'

It is common, since the Georgians are out of favour, for critics to insist of any Georgian poet they admire that he did not really

a This is the same stable rural England that Forster symbolizes in the country house Howards End. It is the Schlegels who appreciate the worth of this place and are its true heirs; but the Wilcoxes who own it.

belong to the movement. Professor Pinto writes that Robert
Graves 'really had no connection with the Georgian fold';[40]
David Daiches insists that the trench poets who appeared in later
issues of the Anthology did not belong there; and a chorus of
critics begins its remarks on D. H. Lawrence's poetry by saying
that he was 'not a Georgian'. In so far as all poets are individuals,
no poet is a Georgian—or a Metaphysical either. But the characteristics which mark off the Georgians from their immediate
predecessors are shared by Lawrence, Graves, Owen, and
Sassoon: a rejection of large themes and of the language of
rhetoric that accompanied them in the nineteenth century; and
an attempt to come to terms with immediate experience, sensuous
or imaginative, in a language close to common speech. The work
of a poet like Wilfred Owen proceeds naturally out of the
Georgian method.[a] The rural prettiness of much Georgian poetry
is the product of sheltered lives, not of deliberate concealment
of facts. And poets like Sassoon, Owen, and Sorley inherit the
honesty, gentleness, and openmindedness of the liberal intellectual movement out of which had come the Georgian anthologies.
Observing suffering that they felt could be avoided, they attacked
stupid patriotism, not with abstract argument, but with a true
presentation of the facts:

> 'If in some smothering dreams, you too could pace
> Behind the wagon that we flung him in,
> And watch the white eyes writhing in his face,
> His hanging face, like a devil's sick of sin;
> If you could hear, at every jolt, the blood
> Come gargling from the froth-corrupted lungs,
> Bitter as the cud
> Of vile, incurable sores on innocent tongues,—
> My friend, you would not tell with such high zest
> To children ardent for some desperate glory,
> The old Lie: Dulce et decorum est
> Pro patria mori.'[41]

a Owen did not appear in the Georgian Anthologies, but he associated himself with the movement. At the end of 1917 he wrote in a
letter: 'I go out of this year a poet, my dear mother, as which I did not
enter it. I am held peer by the Georgians; I am a poet's poet. I am
started'. *Poems of Wilfred Owen*, 1946 (Blunden's memoir, p. 32).

This disgust with the war and horror at its continuance took some of the Georgians beyond mere reporting. Their poetry was motivated by a desire to influence the course of events and to have the war brought to an end. Sassoon records that his war poems gave him 'a strong sense of satisfaction that I was providing a thoroughly caddish antidote to the glorification of "the supreme sacrifice" and such-like prevalent phrases'.[a] And Edmund Blunden writes of Wilfred Owen:

'Owen was preparing himself to the last moment in experience, observation, and composition for a volume of poems, to strike at the conscience of England in regard to the continuance of the war.'[42]

Owen himself insisted:

'Above all I am not concerned with Poetry. My subject is War, and the pity of War. The Poetry is in the pity.'[43]

Thus poetry had again entered the world of public affairs—not in taking up great abstract public themes, but in recording the protest of individual men against the demands put upon them by public sentiment. And though the poetry was limited in its application and often inadequate in technique, though it failed to achieve the universality Yeats achieved in 'Easter 1916', it was nevertheless honest, personal, direct, and its values were humane.

The honesty and directness of Sassoon and Owen found its way only gradually into poetry of the war. The first response was a surge of enthusiasm of which Brooke's sonnets were a part. The older poets rose to the occasion in their habitual manner: Newbolt republished a collection of appropriate poems and almost immediately sold 70,000 copies. ' "The Vigil" is being quoted, sung, recited and reprinted from one end of the country

a *Siegfried's Journey*, p. 19. The fact that, at a time when patriotic feeling had become hysterical, Edward Marsh printed the best of Sassoon's poems despite their 'unpatriotic' sentiment and their use of words like 'syphilitic', is surely further evidence that justice has not been done to him as an anthologist.

to the other' he records in a 1914 letter 'and I have letters of thanks in every post'.[44]

The examples of bad poetry produced in 1914 are endless. In the light of the situation described in Chapter 3, this is to be expected. But there is some point in providing one or two examples of the general quality of the patriotic verse so that the achievement of the Georgians may be seen more clearly in its historical context.

William Watson's address to the German Emperor illustrates the mood and the quality:

> 'Wherefore are men amazed at thee, thou Blot
> On the fair script of Time, thou sceptered smear
> Across the Day? Thou wert divulged full clear—
> Hell's sponsor—long ago! Has earth forgot
> Thy benison on a monster reeking hot
> From shambles bloody as these—thy orient peer,
> Thy heart's mate, and infernal comrade dear?
> His red embrace do men remember not.'[45]

His image of Germany is another example.

> 'Out of the gutters and slums of Hell—
> Disgorged from the vast infernal sewer—
> Vomited forth from a world where dwell
> Childhood, maidenhood, wifehood pure—
> She arose and towered on earth and sea,
> Clothed in her green putridity.'[46]

John Oxenham, fresh in his fame as author of *Bees in Amber: a Little Book of Thoughtful Verse* (see Chapter 3), rose to the occasion of war with *All's Well! Some Helpful Verses for the Dark Days of War*. Any single verse from this book illustrates the quality of the whole, and of a hundred other books:

> 'He died as few men get the chance to die,—
> Fighting to save a world's morality.
> He died the noblest death a man can die,
> Fighting for God, and Right, and Liberty;—
> And such a death is Immortality.'

From the soldiers themselves (usually before their experience of the war was extensive) a similar stream of verse poured into the presses, much of it, like the one below by Willoughby Weaving, in imitation of Brooke's 'If I should die think only this of me' :

> 'If I should haply perish, write me this,
> Except ye nothing write my grave above,
> "He died for England but by England's love" . . .'

Fictional blood poured out in thousands of sonnets and odes, and whatever might have been learned from the first Georgian Anthology was quickly forgotten. 'Art' was not 'life'; soldiering was. It was even suggested that 'culture' had led to corruption in Germany while healthy pursuits like trade, politics, and sport had kept Britain occupied.[47]

Poetry was obviously a useful weapon of propaganda, and 'recruiting verses' were provided by every poet with a sense of public responsibility. Yet it is interesting to note that as this public form of poetry began to be used for the 'writing up' of campaigns, intelligent soldiers rebelled at its dishonesty—not on artistic grounds, but simply because (as poetry of this sort had done for years) it distorted truth for the sake of an optimistic picture. An example of this reaction is found in the *English Review*:[48]

> 'What strikes the soldier is this. Why does a poet write about a military, a desperate military expedition? . . .
>
> 'A few examples. Masefield tackles the Gallipoli fiasco. Mr Kipling is deputed to write a series on naval operations, which he does in his own manner so well that his disquisitions read like fiction, and I believe Sir Henry Newbolt also turned out a poetic rhapsody on the Navy. When the Jutland battle needed "writing up", Mr Winston Churchill got in his knock. Always uncritical, superlative praise: word paint.
>
> '. . . we might have some informed judgments. We might, yet we don't. . . .
>
> '. . . Poets are our strategists, our official "writers up". And this blindness of ours is due to our inexact feeling for words, our hatred of criticism, our refusal to face facts.'

This article is evidence of what Ezra Pound called 'debasing the literary coin to a point where it no longer deceives even the gulls'. As the war continued, more and more people realized the inadequacy of most of the patriotic poetry being written. One notable example of a complete reversal of attitude is Arthur Waugh, the *Quarterly Review*'s poetry critic. In his article already referred to Waugh complained of the lack of 'philosophical content' in Georgian poetry, and called it 'realism running riot'. Two years later[49] he was criticizing the old style of patriotic war poetry because 'It philosophized the situation but did not embody it realistically', and praising the new:

'. . . the chief tendency in English verse for several years before the outbreak of the war had been a tendency towards crude realism, finding its inspiration in themes which had hitherto, perhaps, been considered impossible to the idealizing spirit of poetry. The younger generation, perceiving that the idyllic school of verse had inevitably exhausted its capacities, appeared to have set its heart upon proving that no subject lies intrinsically outside the limits of poetic treatment. . . . The war, therefore, can be said to have offered our young realists the richest possible opportunity for concentrating their art upon the vital moments of life and death.

'. . . [the opportunity] was immediately accepted . . . with the prevalent determination to speak the truth about the ugly things of life, and to strip suffering bare of all concealing veils of sentimentality and pretence. . . .

'The poetry of the future will hardly venture again to sentimentalize an experience which can prompt so sincere and so overwhelming an indignation.'

If a critic formerly so unresponsive to what he had called 'the new realism' could be brought to approve of honesty and clear-sightedness in poetry, many others at this time must also have come to see that 'the true Poets must be truthful'.

The particularization of experience in the work of the new war poets was an immense improvement over the generalizing facility of their imperialist predecessors. But their poems still fall short of the yardstick we have taken—Yeats's 'Easter 1916'. The relationship between the poet and his experience of life is now an honest relationship: here is the poet, and here his experience which he faces without pre-conceptions. It remained yet for other poets—or for at least one other poet—to approach what Yeats had achieved: the transformation of his personal experience into a universal image. As the best post-war poetry moved towards the achievement of T. S. Eliot, the Georgian movement declined rapidly. Its last exponents, shepherded by J. C. Squire in the pages of *The London Mercury*, deserve the scorn that has been poured on the movement as a whole. But we owe the original Georgian movement an acknowledgement it will not receive while critics continue to confuse its beginnings with its decline in the pages of the *Mercury*. Harold Monro, himself one of the original Georgians and a publisher of Georgian poetry, wrote this of the movement in 1920:

'... in its infancy the "Georgian Movement" was uncharacterized by evidence of design, that is, it did not, like other schools, preach or practice a special dogma of poetic art. It was fortuitous and informal. But poets subsequently included in the anthologies devoted much energy to narrowing and hardening what began as a spontaneous co-operative effort. They sought to establish (according to a recent review) "a form of literary tyranny, demanding of its own disciples a complete conformity to certain standards, and seeking to exclude altogether those who refuse to do homage to those laws".'

Edward Marsh's anthologies defined a new relationship between 'Poetry' and 'Life'; and they suggested a new duty for the poet— that he should approach his subject with humility.

REFERENCES

1. *Return to Yesterday*, pp. 44, 45.
2. 'The Last Phase'—*From Dickens to Hardy* (Penguin Books), edited by Boris Ford, p. 389.
3. *Explorations*, p. 172.
4. 'The Last Phase'—*From Dickens to Hardy*, p. 388.
5. ibid., p. 385.

6. *Return to Yesterday*, pp. 85, 86.

7. 'A New Study of English Poetry', *English Review*, January 1912, p. 292.

8. *The Later Life and Letters of Sir Henry Newbolt*, p. 28.

9. ibid., p. 364.

10. 'The Poetry of Mr Alfred Austin', January 1908, p. 173.

11. pp. 173–4. Italics mine.

12. 'Literature as Fine Art', R. A. Scott-James, *English Review*, April 1913.

13. *Lyrical Poems of Alfred Austin*, p. 116.

14. V. de S. Pinto, *Crisis in English Poetry*, p. 32.

15. *Books and Persons*, p. 161. Italics mine.

16. 'Clifton Chapel'.

17. *The Later Life and Letters of Sir Henry Newbolt*, p. 187.

18. 'Minora Sidera'.

19. 'The Vigil'.

20. *English Review*, 'Book Notices', December 1909.

21. *Crisis in English Poetry*, p. 117.

22. 'Book Notices', *English Review*, September 1911.

23. 'The Creation of Taste', ibid., December 1913.

24. ibid.

25. 'Substance in Poetry', ibid., July 1911.

26. *Poetry and the Modern World*, p. 40.

27. 'The New Poetry', *Quarterly Review*, October 1916. See Chapter 3, p. 61.

28. *Collected Poems of Rupert Brooke*, with a memoir by Edward Marsh, liii.

29. ibid., lxvii.

30. ibid., lxviii.

31. *Poetry and Drama*, March 1913, p. 45.

32. *Collected Poems of Rupert Brooke*, lxx.

33. *Georgian Anthology 1911–1912*, p. 106.

34. Robert Graves, *The Common Asphodel*, p. 112.

35. Frank Swinnerton, *The Blue Review*, No. 1, p. 51.

36. *The Common Asphodel*.

37. ibid.

38. 'Reflections on Contemporary Poetry', *The Egoist*, September 1917.

39. *Phoenix*, posthumous papers of D.H.L., p. 305.

40. *Crisis in English Poetry*. Graves's later poetry seems to me to show the Georgian technique brought to perfection.

41. *Poems of Wilfred Owen* (1946), p. 66.

42. ibid., p. 40.

43. ibid.

44. *The Later Life and Letters of Sir Henry Newbolt*, p. 190.

45. *The Man Who Saw and Other Poems Arising Out of the War*, 1917, p.27.

46. *English Review*, December 1915.

47. 'The Ballad of the War', ibid., June 1915.

48. 'Criticism in War', Miles, ibid., December 1916.

49. 'War Poetry', *Quarterly Review*, October 1918.

5

THE SOCIAL FUNCTION OF POETRY

Pound and the Imagists; Eliot

'We are I think getting rid of the glorification of ener-
getic stupidity. . . . The art of the stupid, by the stupid,
for the stupid is not all sufficient. . . . After an intolerable generation we find again this awakening.'

EZRA POUND[1]

'and the news is a long time moving
a long time arriving
through the impenetrable
crystalline, indestructible
ignorance of locality.'

EZRA POUND[2]

FROM this distance critics most often look back at the Imagists
with greater affection than they feel for the Georgians. This is not
because the Imagists as a group displayed greater poetic abilities
or more intelligence; but because the periodicals in which they
appeared provided early opportunities for men like Pound and
Eliot; and because some of the doctrines they inexpertly pro-
pounded developed in the minds of better men to give strength to
what we now recognize as the most significant revolution in
poetry since that initiated by Wordsworth and Coleridge.

What the revolution achieved was first an acknowledgement of
the legitimacy of 'organic form', including where serviceable the
language and rhythms of common speech; and second, a rejection of 'public' themes designed to please a particular audience at

a particular time. Both aspects of this revolution focussed on the poet's relation to his audience, since the general reading public inevitably looked in the new poets for the style, language, and themes it had come to admire in the old. The new poets rejected the Victorian poets and their stylistic heirs as 'rhetorical'—a word which implied (as it does in Yeats's criticism) an unwritten pact by which the poet agreed to confine himself to a particular style and range of subjects, and the audience to respond with uncritical emotion. The Imagists rejected this pact and insisted that they would write the poems that needed to be written, rather than poems a large public would enjoy. The public could go to the devil. In this matter they were not troubled by a confusion of opposing intentions as the Georgians were; but their writing suffered in other ways by its necessary isolation from normal public acclaim.

The Imagist movement began, according to F. S. Flint,[3] in a Soho restaurant in 1909:

'I think what brought the real nucleus of the group together was a dissatisfaction with English poetry as it was then being written. We proposed to replace it by pure *vers libre*; by the Japanese *tanka* and *haikai* . . . by poems like T. E. Hulme's "Autumn", and so on. In all this Hulme was the ringleader. He insisted, too, on absolutely accurate presentation and no verbiage, and he and F. W. Tancred . . . used to spend hours in search of the right phrase. There was also a lot of talk among us about what we called the Image. We were very much influenced by French symbolist poetry.'

Before the start of the war the group had found a new leader (Pound), a periodical (*The Egoist*), and a publisher (Harold Monro). The effectiveness of the movement came to an end, about 1917 when 'two authors, neither engaged in picking the other's pocket, decided that the dilution of *vers libre*, Amygism, Lee Masterism, general floppiness had gone too far and that some counter-current must be set going. . . . Remedy prescribed: "Émaux et Camées" (or the Bay State Hymn Book). Rhyme and regular strophes.

'Result: Poems in Mr Eliot's second volume not contained in his first . . . also Hugh Selwyn Mauberley.'[4]

('Amygism' was Pound's name for Imagism after Amy Lowell had entered the group.)

Very little poetry of worth—apart from Pound's Chinese poems and some of the work of H.D.—had been written in the Imagist style when the group began to lose its energy and voice. But its effect was to help prepare the reading public for the better poetry that followed. It shook up the literary scene, called into question all the dogmas sacred to the established journals and publishers. It followed the Pre-Raphaelite brotherhood, and the Aesthetic movement of the 'nineties—the last unsuccessful insurrection against certain nineteenth-century orthodoxies; and the best motivations and attitudes of the three insurrections lead directly towards the best poetry written since 1920.

Richard Aldington's theory of poetry was a half digested version of Pound's criticism, and his ideas about the relation of the artist and society came second-hand from Yeats's early essays. But he was the chief English spokesman for the group, and in 1915 stated the attitude it consistently adopted towards the poetry-reading public:

'The conditions of modern popular art are so degrading that no man of determined or distinguished mind can possibly adopt them. "What the public wants" are the stale ideas of twenty, or fifty, or even seventy years ago, ideas which any man' of talent rejects at once as banal. It is only the *cliché*, only the stale, the flat, and the profitable in art which finds ready acceptance and eager purchasers; while the exploiters at third hand of original ideas are the only innovators to secure applause. . . . The arts are now divided between popular charlatans and men of talent, who, of necessity, write, think and paint only for each other, since there is no one else to understand them.'[5]

This was a position Pound insisted on, reminding his fellow poets regularly of 'the difference between what is . . . good enough for the public, and what is "good" for the artist, whose only respectable aim is perfection.'[6]

'As for the "eyes of a too ruthless public": damn their eyes. No art ever yet grew by looking into the eyes of the public, ruthless or otherwise. You can obliterate yourself and mirror

God, Nature, or Humanity but if you try to mirror yourself in
the eyes of the public, woe be unto your art.'[7]

He insisted that genuine poetry readers capable of real discrimina-
tion were limited to a few hundred at any one time, and that no
poet whose book demanded 'mental attention' could sell more
than 500 copies.

Together with this rejection of all interest in the existing poetry-
reading public went a violence of statement and an insistence on
the group's superior comprehension of all literary matters. This
was clearly designed to attract attention. 'In dealing with the
"public",' Pound says,[8] 'one has never said enough. There is
nothing but "rubbing it in" that has the slightest effect.' The
Imagists succeeded in attracting attention—particularly in the
United States where Amy Lowell was promoter as well as
practitioner—but the doctrine they preached was often a dilution
or distortion of the perceptions which had prompted Pound and
T. E. Hulme to initiate the movement.

When T. E. Hulme (writing before the First World War)
attacked the Romantic notion 'that man, the individual, is an
infinite reservoir of possibilities', and predicted that a renewal of
poetry must come in the form of 'dry, hard classical verse', he
was in effect attacking the view of the poet as man of sentiment, moralist and prophet. His rejection of the 'personal' (a
deceptive word) in poetry was, if my interpretation is correct, a
rejection of that part of the poet's conscious personality which
tends to present rational accounts of feelings derived from
experience, and to deduce moral positions from them. The
emphasis both Hulme and Pound put on 'art', on the technique
of poetry and the process by which a poem crystallized out of
experience, was a means of escape from an alternation of sentiment and morals in verse. Pound's most important definition—
'An "Image" is that which presents an intellectual and emotional
complex in an instant of time'—is only another attempt to define
the ideal of poetic fusion perceived in Yeats's phrase 'blood,
imagination, intellect, running together', and in Eliot's definition
of the 'undissociated sensibility'. The need for this fusion had
become so great that Pound could add vaguely: 'It is better to
present one Image in a lifetime than to produce voluminous
works.'[9]

The attempt to achieve the 'Image' in poetry was the concern of the poet at the moment of writing. But the Imagists' concern in writing prose was more often to attract attention than to rationalize their literary techniques as clearly as Pound had done in his definition of the Image. 'It is certain that the present chaos will endure', Pound wrote in 1912,

'until the Art of poetry has been preached down the amateur gullet, until there is such a general understanding of the fact that poetry is an art and not a pastime; such a knowledge of technique . . . that the amateurs will cease to try to drown out the masters.'[10]

The chaos was not always diminished by preaching. Pound's Imagist Manifesto, for example, sets out three ideals:

'(i) Direct treatment of the "thing" whether subjective or objective.
'(ii) To use absolutely no word that does not contribute to the presentation.
'(iii) As regarding rhythm: to compose in the sequence of the musical phrase not in the sequence of a metronome.'[11]

This, typically, proposes to eradicate certain stylistic faults, but does not directly fix attention on the fundamental problem implied in his definition of the Image.

Imagist poetry developed as a way of presenting sharp visual perceptions in lines which preserved the emotional experience by a rigid exclusion of all elements of discourse:

> 'The hard sand breaks
> And the grains of it
> Are clear as wine.
>
> 'Far off over the leagues of it,
> The wind
> Playing on the wide shore,
> Piles little ridges
> And the great waves
> Break over it.'[12]

Or in the hands of lesser poets like Aldington and Amy Lowell it became merely a technique for giving sequences of ineffectual prose the appearance of a kind of poetry:

> 'A bird in a plane tree
> Sings a few notes,
> Cadenced and perfect
> They weave into silence.
> The cathedral bell knocks
> One, two, three, and again,
> And then again.
> It is a quiet sound,
> Calling to prayer,
> Hardly scattering the stillness,
> Only making it close in more densely.
> The gardener picks ripe gooseberries
> For the Dean's supper tonight.
> It is very quiet. . . .'[13]

But the importance (in terms of literary history) of the movement should be tested by the achievement of its best practitioners; and a comparison of an Imagist, H.D., with a Georgian, Edward Thomas,[a] demonstrates where the most important motives of the two groups coincided, and where they differed. The Imagists were in general taking Georgian innovations one step further:

[a] Some critics have argued that Edward Thomas was not a Georgian (see, for example, *Edward Thomas* by H. Coombes, p. 10). This I think is only because any critic writing of Thomas at some length wants the poems treated with respect, and knows that for years 'Georgian' has been a term of abuse. It is true that Thomas never appeared in the *Georgian Anthology*, but scarcely any of his poems were published before his death, and then only in book form. Certainly his friends in the later part of his life included many of the Georgian poets; he saw them often, admired their work, and was one of the judges who awarded a prize to Brooke's 'Grantchester'. Thomas hated the rhetoric of patriotic and imperialist poetry (see *Edward Thomas* by Robert P. Eckert, pp. 163–4), and tried to keep the feeling of his own work related always to particular experience. His poems are excellent examples of the common direction of what was best in the original Georgian movement.

(i) 'Naught moves but clouds, and in the glassy lake
   Their doubles and the shadow of my boat.
   The boat itself stirs only when I break
   This drowse of heat and solitude afloat
   To prove if what I see be bird or mote,
   Or learn if yet the shore woods be awake.

   'Long hours since dawn grew,—spread,—and passed on
      high
   And deep below,—I have watched the cool reeds hung
   Over images more cool in imaged sky:
   Nothing there was worth thinking of so long;
   All that the ring-doves say, far leaves among,
   Brims my mind with content thus still to lie.'

                              ('*July*', EDWARD THOMAS)

(ii) 'Whirl up, sea—
    Whirl your pointed pines,
    Splash your great pines
    On our rocks,
    Hurl your green over us—
    Cover us with your pools of fir.'

                              ('H.D.')

Both poets have attempted to realize with precision one intensely
experienced moment in which the physical situation suggested
something beyond itself. In both there has been an intense reaction against generalization and abstraction: if there is 'significance' in the experience it must emerge by recreation rather than
by reminiscence and rationalization. Thomas's poem is des-
criptively, but not extensively, discursive. H.D. goes a step
further: her poem is a dramatic statement which provides a
single non-discursive image; the 'I' which Thomas uses is present
only implicitly in H.D.'s poem. The most obvious difference is
the difference in form. Thomas's poem is regularly rhymed, and
though his lines run on with a variation of emphasis, five iambic
feet can be counted in each. This difference is in one respect
deceptive. H.D.'s poem can be seen as three lines of blank verse,
not in regular iambics, but made up of five clear speech stresses
as some of the lines in Shakespeare's last plays are:

Whírl up, sea—/Whírl your pointed pines,
Splásh your greát pínes On our rócks,/Húrl
your gréen óver us—/Cóver us with your póols of fír.

Verbally each poem is simple and unpretentious; but in
Thomas's there are phrases which the Imagist would reject as
'cliché'—'naught moves', 'far leaves among'—phrases which
lead one away from the particular experience into the limbo of
half-realized poems where hearts beat, birds sing, flowers bloom,
and tears fall, all to no purpose. On the other hand there is a
single line elevating the whole poem a little beyond the commonplace:

'Nothing there was worth thinking of so long.'

—the success of which might be explained in part by the fact that
there is an acknowledgement of the world and of values beyond
the poem implicit in the ironic self-mockery; and in part by the
slight ambiguity which permits the suggestion that 'nothing', as
a subject for contemplation, was indeed 'worth thinking of so
long'. From H.D.'s single moment of experience the world of
values is totally excluded; but the rare point is achieved at which
discourse can disappear without communication being elimin-
ated. An experience is suggested in which the persona behind
the poem lies in a forest while wind moves the pines overhead.
The correspondence between the pine forest and the sea is one
of shapes, colours, and above all (implied, not stated) sounds—
the sound of waves breaking and of wind in pines.

Both the Georgian poet and the Imagist poet in their purest
poems aim at the expression of precise emotions or states of
mind. In the case of these two poems H.D. is more successful.
Another pair of poems will suggest further the achievements of
the two groups—and their limitations—in relation to the poets
who preceded them:

(i) 'Harry, you know at night
The larks in Castle Alley
Sing from the attic's height
As if the electric light
Were the true sun above a summer valley:
Whistle, don't knock, tonight.

'I shall come early, Kate:
And we in Castle Alley
Will sit close out of sight
Alone and ask no light
Of lamp or sun above a summer valley:
Tonight I can stay late.'

('Tonight', EDWARD THOMAS)

(ii) 'Thou art come at length
More beautiful than any cool god
In a chamber under Lycia's far coast,
Than any high god who touches us not
Here in the seeded grass.
Aye, than Argestes
Scattering the broken leaves.'

('Sitalkas', 'H.D.')

Again there is in each case a paring down to the essentials of a situation which is intended to convey the particular emotion of the poem—the Imagist poet taking the process further than the Georgian. In Thomas's poem we overhear a short dialogue in which we learn the names of the two personae, the place where they intend to meet, and certain facts about that place. In H.D.'s we are inside the mind of one of two people. The poem offers a musical equivalent for a state of mind into which only two substantial facts are permitted to enter. In this the 'clichés' which the Imagists substituted for older 'clichés' are evident; the bag of assorted antiquities is an unsatisfactory substitute for the concretely realized situation on which Edward Thomas has constructed his poem.

These poems are examples of Georgianism and Imagism at their purest—that is, they are poems in which the common impulses driving the poets away from certain habits of mind and towards others were allowed to form the style. But often in the case of the Imagists a pose consciously adopted in relation to the poetry-reading public confused the poet and distracted him from adequate realization of his own theory and style. The following extract from an article by Richard Aldington[14] is a good example of an Imagist poet failing to realize fully the problem he is dealing with—and failing partly because he is more concerned with attracting attention, with 'preaching the art of poetry down the amateur gullet', than with coming to terms with his subject. The passage is interesting, too, because a crude, embryonic version of Eliot's theory of the 'objective correlative' (another way of escape from the 'personal') can be seen in it:

'We convey an emotion by presenting the object and circumstances of that emotion, without comment. For example we do not say "O how I admire that beautiful, that exquisite, that—25 more adjectives—woman", or "O exquisite, O beautiful, O 25 more adjectives woman, let us spoon you for ever", but we present that woman, we make an Image of her, we make the scene convey the emotion. . . . A hardness of cut stone. No slop, no sentimentality. When people say Imagist poems are "too hard", "like a white marble monument", we chuckle; we know that we have done something good.'

The aggressiveness apparent here, the note of 'telling the Philistines a few home truths', enters the poetry too. Yeats, faced with the same problems in his relations with the poetry-reading public, kept all the cruder conceptions of the poet as member of a 'favoured few' out of his poetry, only allowing it as an occasional weapon in his prose. Pound on the other hand was always willing to forget pure Imagist doctrine for the purpose of attacking the readers of Tennysonian 'Rhetoric' with a rhetoric of his own:

> 'Will the people accept them?
>   (i.e. these songs).
> As timorous wench from a centaur
>   (or a centurion)
> Already they flee howling with terror.
> Will they be touched with the truth?
>   Their virgin stupidity is untemptable.
> I beg you, my friendly critics,
> Do not set about to procure me an audience.
>
> 'I mate with my free kind among the crags;
>   the hidden recesses
> Have heard the echo of my heels
>   in the cool light,
>   in the darkness.'[15]

Another form this attitude took can be seen in the city poems in which the sensitive intellectual finds himself in contact with an insensitive urban population:

> 'A row of eyes,
> Eyes of greed, of pitiful blankness, of plethoric
>   complacency,
> Immobile,
> Gaze, stare at one point,
> At my eyes.

> 'Antagonism,
> Disgust,
> Immediate antipathy,
> Cut my brain, as a sharp dry reed
> Cuts a finger.

> 'I surprise the same thought
> In the brasslike eyes:

> ' *"What right have you to live?"* '[16]

> (RICHARD ALDINGTON)

Or again, the kind of writing in which the poet presents himself as one of a group who know the truth about the fundamental problems of life—a truth which eludes all but the elect:

> 'Have I spoken too much or not enough of love?
> Who can tell?
> But we who do not drug ourselves with lies
> Know, with how deep pathos, that we have
> Only the warmth and beauty of the world
> Before the blackness of the unending gloom.'[17]

> (RICHARD ALDINGTON)

For Pound, the assaults of the *Egoist* on the literate public did not go far enough. Something of greater explosive power was required if the English literary world was to be shaken at its foundations in the way he hoped. For this purpose *BLAST* was instituted. 'I can use nothing', Pound said in a letter, 'which is not definitely an insult to the public library, the general reader, the weekly press.' *BLAST* announced itself with a mixture of generous moderation and crude simplification:

'We want to make in England not a popular art, not a revival of lost folk art, or a romantic fostering of such unactual conditions, but to make individuals. . . .

'We are against the glorification of "the People" as we are against snobbery. It is not necessary to be an outcast bohemian, to be unkempt or poor, any more than it is necessary to be rich or handsome, to be an artist. . . .

'The "Poor" are detestable animals! They are only picturesque or amusing to the sentimentalist or the romantic! The "Rich" are bores without a single exception, *en tant que riches!*

'We want those simple and great people found everywhere.

'*BLAST* presents an art of individuals!'[18]

The 'enemies of culture' were attacked with breath-taking vigour. *The Times*, for example, Pound addressed as

'You slut-bellied obstructionist,
    You sworn foe of free speech and good letters,
    You fungus, you continuous gangrene . . .'

The money-makers and usurers also received abuse:

'Come Let us on with the new deal,
    Let us be done with Jews and Jobbery,
    Let us SPIT on those who fawn on the Jews for their money,
    Let us out to the pastures.'[a]

'Romance' was another target for attack, together with 'every form that poetry of a former condition of life, no longer existing, has foisted upon us.' Against these were set the IMAGE, 'the primary pigment of poetry', and, more obscurely, the VORTEX, 'the point of maximum energy'. The 'favoured few' were courted in terms which succeeded only in invoking another form of 'romance':

[a] Pound allows the Jew a capital J, a courtesy which Eliot has thought dispensable.

> 'Let me be free of pavements,
> Let me be free of printers.
> Let come beautiful people
> Wearing raw silk of good colour,
> Let come the graceful speakers,
> Let come the ready of wit,
> Let come the gay of manner the insolent and the exulting;
> We speak of burnished lakes,
> And of dry air, as clear as metal.'

That Pound thought of the 'beautiful people' as his 'brother artists' can be seen by comparing these lines with an extract from his memoir of Gaudier-Brzeska (p. 148) written a year later:

> '. . . we are indissolubly united against all non-artists and half-artists by our sense of this fundamental community, this unending adventure towards "arrangement", this search for the equation of eternity.'

—a remark which has that ring of 'aestheticism' about it that has consistently accompanied the twentieth-century poet's insistence on his right of independence from his audience.

In this latter respect the line from the 'nineties through to the younger Eliot is unbroken. This is not to say that Eliot wished to eliminate whatever moral function poetry had for its audience; but that in the writing of poetry he was (like all the poets of this tradition) in search of freedom to develop a synthesis of the two emphases of thought which we refer to abstractly as 'aesthetics' and 'morals'—a search that made necessary an attack on certain public expectations and demands which, if listened to, prevented the synthesis taking place. Poetics (Hugh Kenner says of the literature against which Pound and Eliot were in reaction) had

> 'given way to rhetoric. *The poet in a dialectical milieu is conscious of an audience to be influenced rather than a poem to be made. . . .*'[19]

The problem was to find a man capable of rationalizing and stating adequately those group intuitions which were healthy and capable of development. Pound in much of his criticism was too impatient to realize these exactly, though he never failed to distinguish accurately between the good and the mediocre among his contemporaries. A large amount of his writing—like that in *BLAST*—was publicity, nothing more. Aldington realized that the movement was heir to the Aesthetes of the 'nineties, but he was not capable of the occasional flashes of insight that illuminated Pound's best prose. It was not until Eliot began to write criticism that a number of ideas which had existed, half-realized, in the minds of the literary avant-garde for a number of years, found adequate formulation. The essential unity of impulse can, nevertheless, be clearly detected in the prose of the three men:

'[I quarrel with] that infamous remark of Whitman's about poets needing an audience.' (Pound.)[20]

'In the nineties popularity was (rightly) held to be a reproach.' (Aldington.)[21]

'It is wrong of Mr Kipling to address a large audience; but it is a better thing than to address a small one. The only better thing is to address the one hypothetical Intelligent Man who does not exist and who is the audience of the artist.' (Eliot.)[22]

(Eliot's remark, it should be noted, appeared shortly after the publication of *The Wild Swans at Coole*, containing 'The Fisherman' in which Yeats states his determination to write for 'A man who does not exist,/A man who is but a dream'.)

'I believe in technique as the test of a man's sincerity.' (Pound.)[23]

'It is recorded of [Dowson] that his theories of poetry were solely technical; and that proves, if proof be necessary, his authentic character as an artist.' (Aldington.)[24]

'[The task of the artist is] a task in the same sense as the making of an efficient engine or the turning of a jug or a table leg.' (Eliot.)[25]

There can be no doubt that in this last quotation Eliot meant it was the poet's job to concern himself with the *process*, the making of his poem, and with little else. More will be said about this in the next chapter; but it must be insisted that what Eliot implies here is the artist's consciousness of bringing something into *being*, and not of conveying a *meaning*. 'The theory of "art for art's sake",' he writes in 1930, 'is still valid insofar as it can be taken as an exhortation to the artist to stick to his job.'[26] Thus the position is completed by a rejection of the idea that the poet should think of his poem as an instrument while he is writing it:

'Art never asks anybody to do anything, or to think anything, or to be anything. It exists as the trees exist, you can admire, you can sit in the shade, you can pick bananas, you can cut firewood, you can do as you jolly well please.' (Pound)[27]

'I do not deny that art may be affirmed to serve ends beyond itself; but art is not required to be aware of these ends, and indeed performs its function, whatever that function may be, according to various theories of value, much better by indifference to them.' (Eliot)[28]

As an obvious extension of this statement we may remark that if 'art' is not required to be aware of the ends it serves, neither is the artist required to be aware of them. It is this position which allows Eliot to concede that different or even contradicting interpretations of the same poem may be equally correct: one critic is picking bananas, another cutting firewood; the artist's job is only to plant and nurture the trees.

In the immediate post-war years the literary scene in England was confused. The few good poets among the Georgians who had survived the war (Robert Graves and Walter de la Mare, for example) ceased to think of themselves as members of a group. In the pages of *The London Mercury* J. C. Squire, John Freeman, Edward Shanks, W. J. Turner, and others—'the Squirearchy' as Osbert Sitwell was to call them—maintained an enfeebled Georgian style, setting themselves resolutely against 'modernism'. (The current reputation of the Georgian movement as a whole stems largely, I think, from a failure to distinguish between these men and their predecessors.) 'All that is left now of the Georgian poets,' Middleton Murry remarked in 1919,[29] 'is what we may call the family features.' The poetic technique, revolutionary in 1910, was already reactionary by 1920.

Imagism exhausted itself in a shorter time, and diminished to insignificance when Pound and Eliot decided that vers libre had gone far enough. In England another group of poets, led by Edith, Osbert, and Sacheverell Sitwell, took up the banner of 'modernism':

'*Form* is determined by the emotion which requires expression.
'*Corollary:* Form is not an unchanging mould into which any emotions can be poured.
'By *vision* we mean the recognition of emotions possessing an aesthetic value . . . of course we have long passed the day when aesthetic creation demands an ethical sanction . . . .
'*Value* is determined by relation to the artist's conception of absolute beauty. . . .
'This question only remains doubtful: Does significant expression end with the artist's satisfaction, or should it necessarily re-create the artist's vision in another mind? At any rate a relative question, for there is not equality of aesthetic perception, and the artist can always claim an aristocracy.'[30]

And Frank Rutter's 'Nine Propositions' in the same journal[31] included

'Vital art work is always controversial and displeasing to the public.'

A war of quite astonishing triviality raged between the two principal literary camps. Osbert Sitwell attacked the enemies of "modernism" in satirical verse no more subtle than Pound at his worst, and less vigorous:

> 'The General says
> He dislikes poetry most.
> Kipling is different
> He is a Man-of-the-World.
> But the General says
> That if he could get hold
> Of one of those long-haired
> Conscientious Objectors

Who write things
That don't even rhyme . . .'[32]

'Our sons
And brothers
Went forth to fight,
To kill certain things—
"All this poetry and rubbish"—
We said
We will not buy "Art and Letters".'[33]

In the *Monthly Chapbook* (No. 29) he satirized *The London Mercury*, its editor J. C. Squire, and its contributors ('the squirearchy'), with a poem entitled 'The Jolly Old Squire or Way Down in Georgia':

'Meanwhile the nature crew
Hymn every bird that ever croaked or flew.'

Squire retaliated with a lumbering satirical story, 'The Man Who Wrote Free Verse'[34] which included the following explanation of the new poetry:

'It's a kind of hideous little underworld, the kind of thing you see when you lift up a large stone and see disgusting insects, beetles, and centipedes, scuttling about. They dislike daylight too. The second rate have discovered the trick of incomprehensibility in our time; the trick of bogus audacity has always been known.'

One English branch of this 'hideous little underworld' appeared annually from 1916 to 1920 in *Wheels*, an anthology which attracted attention at first because so many of its contributors had interesting parents—a Huxley, three Sitwells, an Hon. Wyndham Tennant, a daughter of Sir Herbert Beerbohm Tree, a daughter of Sir Bache and Lady Cunard. 'The names speak for themselves', the *Observer* commented; the *Sketch* correctly predicted 'their names are enough to secure a second edition'. The anthology savoured of a plot cooked up in the spacious boredom of the nursery:

'Oh, Afternoons, Afternoons . . .
Snug rectories where no foot crunches
The sleek gravel except the pad-paw of baboons.'

(ALDOUS HUXLEY)

'The people that pass
Seem castles of glass,
The old and the good
Giraffes of blue wood.'

(EDITH SITWELL)

There was a fashionable disillusion—associated with the phrase 'this generation'. Iris Tree complained:

'The adored, wild, strange, irresistible,
How they fail one at the last!'

and added (perhaps remembering similar poems by Aldington):

'People—
Men and women with laughable tragic faces
Winking at love,
Treading our songs and illusions
Under petulant feet.'

Osbert Sitwell toyed with the life-is-death death-is-life 'paradox', which Eliot was later to make respectable:

'Their tears ran dry when they were in the womb,
For, entering life—they found it was their tomb!'

But the immaturity of much that went into *Wheels* is perhaps best displayed by the retaliation of its editor, Edith Sitwell, on the author of an unfavourable review. An open letter on the subject began 'Though the above is unsigned, I detect in it the traces, less of the cloven hoof than of a certain wooden head'; it went on to identify the reviewer as a certain Miss Jones (who belonged in the Lyons Popular rather than in literary circles), and concluded:

'Frankly, darling, What a stinker!' Later issues of *Wheels* included Miss Sitwell's attacks on 'Hoity-Toity Topsy Jones', and a cross under which was written

R.I.P. Topsy Jones

Who died defending 'A Common Cause'

(Editor's Note: *very*)

1919

T. S. Eliot, Pound has said,[35] 'displayed great tact, or enjoyed good fortune in arriving in London at a particular date with a formed style of his own'. It should be added that he displayed his strength and independence of mind in retaining and developing that style in the literary chaos existing at the time. Between 1912 and 1918 new poetry had poured from English publishing houses in a steady stream. Poets united into groups according to theories or rejection of theories—Traditionalists, Georgians, Imagists, Futurists, Impressionists, Vorticists. The possibility of any poet rising to a dominant position must have seemed as remote as the thought that any critic might succeed in discovering basic principles on which a majority of his contemporaries could agree.

In his attitude to the public Eliot aligned himself with the Imagists—though in this as in all else his opinions were more flexible, more maturely thought out, and more brilliantly stated than those of his fellow poets. His statement that 'the artist' should write for 'the one hypothetical Intelligent Man who does not exist' has already been quoted. Like the Imagists, Eliot held this position together with a belief in the need for attack on the public. But he displayed a sense of social responsibility which was totally absent in lesser poets like Aldington:

'What we want is to disturb and alarm the public: to upset its dependence on Shakespeare, Nelson, Wellington and Sir Isaac Newton; to point out that at any moment the relation of a modern Englishman to Shakespeare may be discovered to be that of a modern Greek to Aeschylus. . . . That the forces of deterioration are a large crawling mass, and the forces of development half a dozen men . . . for if our predecessors cannot teach us to write better than themselves, they will surely teach us to write worse . . .

'We must insist upon the importance of intelligent criticism.'[36]

Eliot succeeded in disturbing and alarming—first in the pages of the *Egoist*, later in the *Athenaeum*. Many of the articles have not been reprinted, probably because they are exercises in literary politics rather than responsible criticism in the strictest sense. But they represent an important shift in the balance of literary power: 'modernism' had at last acquired a voice which could not be ignored and which could not be shrugged off as irresponsible or immature. No critical commonplace, old or new, was safe from inspection; and reputations unquestioned in the popular mind were all the more likely to suffer diminution—as in the following examples of killing two birds with one stone:

'I cannot see the resemblance to Tennyson which people often see in Georgian poetry . . . Tennyson was careful in his syntax; and moreover his adjectives usually have a definite meaning . . . And Tennyson had a brain (a large dull brain like a farmhouse clock) which saved him from triviality.'[37]

'Because we have never learned to criticize Keats, Shelley and Wordsworth (poets of assured though modest merit) Keats, Shelley and Wordsworth punish us from their graves with the annual scourge of the Georgian Anthology.'[38]

'I have seen the forces of death with Mr Chesterton at their head on a white horse. Mr Pound, Mr Joyce and Mr Lewis write living English; one does not realize the awfulness of death until one meets the living language.'[39]

The 'modernists' were not allowed to preen themselves either. Eliot's 'Reflections on Vers Libre',[40] with its insistence that 'no verse is free for the man who wants to do a good job', angered the Imagists by its careful weighing and testing of their theories. Another example of Eliot's independence is his essay 'The Lesson of Baudelaire' printed in the *Tyro*,[41] a publication for the *avant garde* edited by Wyndham Lewis. After the usual attack on the triviality of the Georgian enemy, Eliot concludes:

'On the other hand, the poets who consider themselves most opposed to Georgianism, and who know a little French, are mostly such as could imagine the Last Judgement only as a lavish display of Bengal Lights, Roman candles, catherine wheels, and inflammable fire balloons. *Vous*, hypocrite lecteur . . .'

It is certain that Eliot's prose made people sooner aware that he was a man to be taken seriously than would have been the case had he written only poetry. The initial blankness of the reaction to his poetry in official literary circles is exemplified by the notice of *Prufrock* in the *Athenaeum*.[42] The title *Prufrock and other Observations* itself seems ironical placed on the 'Notice of New Books' page between *Behind the Firing Line and other Poems of War* and *A Child of Nature and other Verse*. On the same page Willoughby Weaving is praised for 'purity of diction and well chiselled lines'. The full notice of Eliot's book reads:

'Certain of the pieces in this collection have already appeared in print. The verses possess a quality which, for want of a more apt name, we may call Beardsleyesque.'

The publication of *The Sacred Wood* drew attention to the mind behind this 'Beardsleyesque' quality, but for a time this only served to intensify the feeling that Eliot as a poet was perversely difficult. With a genuine effort of appreciation John Middleton Murry could only see him (in *Ara Vos Prec*) as 'the chameleon who changes colour infinitely, and every change is protective'.[43] 'The Waste Land' only seemed to make the difficulties greater. 'Here is Mr Eliot', the *Times Literary Supplement* complained,

'a dandy of the choicest phrase, permitting himself blatancies like "the young man carbuncular". Here is a poet capable of a style more refined than that of any of his generation, parodying without taste or skill. . . . Here is a writer to whom originality is almost an inspiration borrowing the greater number of his best lines, creating hardly any himself.'[44]

J. C. Squire[45] confessed that he was 'unable to make head or tail of it' and added:

'There is a vagrant string of drab pictures which abruptly change, and these are interspersed with memories of literature, lines from old poets, and disconnected ejaculations. . . . A grunt would have served as well; what is language but communication, or art but selection and arrangement? I give it up; but it is a pity that a man who can write as well as Mr Eliot writes in this poem should be so bored with existence that he doesn't mind what comes next or who understands it.'

F. L. Lucas[46] found no difficulty in comprehending the poem. 'Miss Weston is clearly a theosophist', he wrote, 'and Mr Eliot's poem might be a theosophist tract'. But philosophy was not poetry, and he found it

'hard not to regret the way in which modern writers of real creative power abandon themselves to the fond illusion that they have philosophic gifts and a weighty message to deliver to the world as well.'

John Middleton Murry (who had recently dismissed Yeats's *Wild Swans at Coole* as 'Mr Yeats's Swan Song') assured readers of the *Adelphi*[47] that no one would read 'The Waste Land' in fifty years' time. Typically, Harold Monro seems to have been the only editor to insist that the work was 'as near to poetry as our generation is capable of reaching'.[48]

It is not surprising to find Eliot writing in his 'Brief Treatise on the Criticism of Poetry':

'Let the public ask itself why it has never heard of the poems of T. E. Hulme or Isaac Rosenberg, and why it has heard of the poems of Lady Precocia Pondœuf and has seen a photograph of the nursery in which she wrote them. . . . If only it were possible to abate this nuisance of reviewing, we might hope for some improvement of the condition of verse. . . . Let us come to look back upon reviewing as a barbarous habit of a half-civilized age.'[a]

[a] *Monthly Chapbook*, No. 9, March 1920. Eliot was not, of course, himself guiltless in this matter of reviewing. In his review of Yeats's *The Cutting of an Agate* for example (*Athenaeum*, 4 July 1919), Eliot viciously mis-uses his talents to undermine the reputation of the greatest English-speaking poet alive and writing at this time.

But the reviewers of Eliot's early poetry were fighting a rear-guard action. The Great War, followed by economic depression, opened cracks in the defence of literary conservatism. Eliot's criticism helped to prepare the ground for his poetry, and the 'Chinese Wall' of popular poetic discursiveness had already been shaken by a number of earlier attacks. By the early 1930's 'modernism' ceased to be 'modernism' and could safely be called poetry, a field in which Eliot was a dominant figure. The support of men like F. R. Leavis and I. A. Richards in the universities, and of the New Critics in the United States, made counter-attack impossible. The revolutionary committee settled comfortably into the respectability of government.

It should be possible at this point to see the more extreme examples of 'aesthetic' attitudes in Eliot's early criticism as part of a delicately balanced relationship between the poet and his audience. To an audience trained to criticize a poem by the 'ideas' that can be extracted from it rather than for its value as a total complex unit, the poet can only insist that there are *no* ideas, that the poem has a being but no meaning. Thus Eliot, in his early criticism, insists that Henry James had so fine a mind that no idea could violate it; that neither Shakespeare nor Dante did any thinking on his own; that 'the poet makes poetry, the metaphysician makes metaphysics, the bee makes honey, the spider secretes a filament; you can hardly say that any of these agents believes: he merely does'.[49] Together with this critical rejection of conscious 'thought' runs an attempt to achieve a technique for the writing of poetry by which the partisan tendencies of the rational will have only secondary importance.

But once a new audience has begun to appear, an audience willing to take modern poetry on its own terms rather than on the terms of Kipling or Henry Newbolt, the aesthetic attitudes begin to relax. The poet wishes, in poetry almost as much as in criticism, to write positively—to affirm. This is certainly true of Yeats. And there is a gradual shift in Eliot too—from the symbolist towards the discursive in poetry, from the aesthetic towards the moral in criticism, and generally from the esoteric towards the popular. These are *tendencies* only, and Eliot, like Yeats, has not always satisfactorily resolved the oppositions in his criticism. I shall try to show in my final chapters that he does not quite resolve them in his poetry either, and that this keeps his work short of the complete success achieved in the finest poems of Yeats.

It was Pound's criticism that has provided Eliot with a means of retaining the insistence that 'art never asks anyone to do anything, or think anything, or be anything. It exists . . .', together with a claim for the social importance of poetry. 'Has literature a function in the state?' Pound asks in 1928[50] and answers promptly 'It has.'

'And this function is *not* the coercing or emotionally persuading, or bullying or suppressing people into acceptance of any one set or six sets of opinions as opposed to any other one set or half-dozen sets of opinions.

'It has to do with the clarity and vigour of "any and every" thought and opinion. It has to do with maintaining the very cleanliness of the tools, the health of the very matter of thought itself. . . . The individual cannot think and communicate his thought, the governor and legislator cannot act effectively, or frame his laws, without words, and the solidity and validity of these words is the care of the damned and despised *litterati*. When their work goes rotten . . . the whole machinery of social and of individual thought . . . goes to pot.'

This is an extension of Pound's earlier statements on the subject of morals and art, which included[51] 'good art, however "immoral" it is, is wholly a thing of virtue. . . . By good art I mean art that bears true witness, that is wholly precise.' In 1934 he adds that 'writers are the voltometers and steamgauges of the nation's intellectual life. They are the registering instruments, and if they falsify their report there is no end to the harm they can do.'

Eliot moved gradually towards a similar insistence. In *The Use of Poetry* . . .[52] he does not commit himself very far in the matter of the poet's usefulness. After admitting that 'every poet would like to be able to think that he had some direct social utility' he goes on to separate this utility from that of 'the theologian, the preacher, the economist, the sociologist, or anybody else', and to see the function which would satisfy the poet as 'something of a popular entertainer' conveying 'the pleasures of poetry' to a large audience, ideally in the theatre.

In 1940[53] he is more specific, and closer to Pound. The writer

'is useful, in the degree of his greatness, to all those who speak the same language, even if they never hear of him . . . he keeps the language from deteriorating or getting ossified.'

The point (present in various forms in Eliot's prose) that 'a living language, being alive, can die' is made again. It is the business of the writer as artist to see that the language retains its vitality. His preoccupation is 'a preoccupation with words which is at the same time an exploration of subtleties of thought and feeling'.

'So the writer as artist is the most important single factor in preserving, refreshing and developing the language . . . a people and its language will advance or deteriorate together . . . it is the capacity of a people to produce the writer as artist that prevents a people from sinking to a condition where a short scale of farmyard noises will provide all the vehicle it needs for expression and communication.'

There is some confusion between *symptoms* and *causes* in this view of the artist's role, as there is in Eliot's fuller statement of it in 'The Social Function of Poetry'.[54] What is relevant here is that an escape hatch has been found out of an old trap: poetry is neither 'public' as in the moralist tradition, nor 'private' as in the aesthete's. In 'The Social Function of Poetry', for example, Eliot writes:

'We must avoid being seduced into one or the other of two extreme opinions. The first is that it is simply the value of the *ideas* expressed in a poem which gives value to the poetry. The other is that the ideas, the beliefs, of the poet do not matter at all.'

This does not come to terms with the problem of a unified critical apprehension; but it avoids both the heresies which most commonly follow from a division of interests. Thus Eliot is able, without any specific reference to a *moral* function for the poet, to see his usefulness as something extending to the whole nation, whether or not the nation is generally conscious of its writers. This, too, is an idea derived from Pound:

'It does not matter whether the author desire the good of the race or acts merely from personal vanity. The thing is mechanical in action. In proportion as his work is exact, i.e. true to human consciousness and the nature of man, as it is exact in formulation of desire, so it is durable and so it is "useful"; I mean it maintains the precision and clarity of thought, not merely for the benefit of a few dilettantes and "lovers of literature", but maintains the health of thought outside literary circles and in non-literary existence, in general individual and communal life.'[55]

Together with this theory of the social usefulness of poetry, Eliot develops a greater interest in his audience. He retains the independence which forbids that anything should be changed in order to please an audience, and his willingness to shock where shock tactics are useful. But he renounces as a kind of defeatism Q. D. Leavis's idea that an 'armed and conscious minority' can be the only audience for a great writer in his own lifetime. This is a situation that the poet can only accept with reluctance,

'for we should all like to think that our poetry might be read and declaimed in the public house, the forecastle and the shipyard.'[56]

Like Yeats, who imagined his ideal reader as the 'wise and simple' fisherman, Eliot fears most the half-educated audience— those who know only enough literature to have simple and fixed ideas about what poems ought to be; and his reference (in *The Use of Poetry* . . .) to the advantages of having an illiterate audience is entirely serious since, for him, a poem has always been an emotional unit in which the surface 'meaning', though it certainly exists, is only 'to satisfy one habit of the reader, to keep his mind diverted and quiet while the poem does its work on him'. The illiterate auditor's response would be less complete than that of the trained mind; but it might be an unmixed response (a 'unified sensibility' is perhaps implied) unattainable in the minds of 'the half-educated and the ill-educated' who insist upon asking 'what does it mean?' before the poem has been allowed to do its work.[57]

Eliot rejects, too, any attempt to look to one social class or educated minority for the poet's following. The composition of the poet's audience has, he writes in 1941,

'no relation to any social and economic stratification of society. The audience for the more highly developed, even for the more esoteric kinds of poetry is recruited from every level: often the uneducated find them easier to accept than do the half educated.'[58]

Thus in his later attitude to his audience Eliot avoids two heresies: that of the aesthete, and that of the popular rhetorician. The true poet, he implies, does not disperse his audience by denying its existence and his need that it should exist; nor does he attract an audience by saying the things it wants most to hear, and claiming special status for his 'ideas'. But while these two heresies are avoided, Eliot's specific discussion of the function of poetry remains somewhat confused. The poet's job is 'to keep clean the tools of thought'; and it is never clear how the poet's insistence on precision in his own work can in any important way affect the society as a whole. The failure of a society's poets may indeed be a symptom of general decline; it is difficult to see how their success can be a *cause* of general health.

What Eliot fails to say directly (perhaps because he knows too well the possibilities of misunderstanding) is that poetry as he conceives it *has* an intrinsic 'moral' function, but one which is different from 'morals' as they are usually understood; different, certainly, from the moral value attached to poetry in the nineteenth century. A study of those parts of his criticism which indicate most clearly his idea of the nature of poetic composition, will lead directly to an understanding of this elusive concept of poetry's moral value; for the 'value' resides in the accuracy of the 'Image'. It thus concerns the second line of the triangle discussed in my Introduction—that which runs between the poet and the world of experience which is his subject-matter.

REFERENCES

1. *Gaudier Brzeska*, 1916.
2. *Canto* LXXXII.
3. 'The History of Imagism', *Egoist*, 1 May 1915.
4. Ezra Pound, *Criterion*, July 1932.
5. 'Some Reflections on Ernest Dowson', *Egoist*, 1 March 1915.
6. *Letters*, p. 98.
7. ibid., p. 37.
8. ibid., p. 172.
9. *Literary Essays*, p. 4 (1913).
10. ibid., p. 10.
11. ibid., p. 3 (1913).
12. H.D., *Egoist*, 2 February 1914.
13. Amy Lowell, *Egoist*, 16 February 1914.
14. 'Modern Poetry and the Imagists', *Egoist*, 1 April 1914.
15. 'Tenzone', *Egoist*, 15 August 1913.
16. *Egoist*, 1 March 1915.
17. *Art and Letters*, vol. II, no. 1, 1918.
18. No. 1, 20 June 1914, 'Long Live the Vortex'.
19. *The Poetry of Ezra Pound*, p. 72. Italics mine.
20. *Letters*, p. 161 (written 1917).
21. 'Some Reflections on Ernest Dowson', *Egoist*, 1 March 1915.
22. *Athenaeum*, 9 May 1919.
23. *Literary Essays*, p. 9 (written 1918).
24. 'Some Reflections on Ernest Dowson'.
25. *Selected Essays*, p. 114 (written 1924).
26. ibid., p. 442.
27. *Literary Essays*, p. 46 (written 1913).
28. *Selected Essays*, p. 24 ('The Function of Criticism', 1923).
29. *Athenaeum*, 11 April 1919.
30. Herbert Read *Art and Letters*, vol. I, no. 3, January 1918. 'Definitions towards a modern theory of poetry'.
31. Vol. II, p. 52.
32. *The Apple*, vol. 1, no. 1., p. 33.
33. *Art and Letters*, vol. II, no. 1, 1918.
34. *The London Mercury*, vol. 10, no. 56, June 1924.
35. *Criterion*, July 1932—a note on Harold Monro.
36. *Egoist*, May 1918. 'Observations' by 'T.S. Apteryx'.
37. ibid., 'Verse Pleasant and Unpleasant'.
38. ibid., 'Observations'.
39. ibid.
40. *New Statesman*, 3 March 1917.

41. No. 1, 1922.
42. December 1917—before Middleton Murry became editor.
43. *Athenaeum*, 20 February 1920.
44. 20 September 1923.
45. *The London Mercury*, vol. III, no. 48, October 1923.
46. *New Statesman*, 3 November 1923.
47. Vol. III, no. 7.
48. *Monthly Chapbook*, no. 34, February 1923.
49. *Selected Essays*, p. 138.
50. *Literary Essays*, Ezra Pound, p. 21.
51. ibid., p. 44.
52. p. 154 (1933).
53. 'The writer as artist', *The Listener*, 28 November 1940.
54. *Adelphi*, vol. 21, no. 4, September 1945.
55. Pound, *Literary Essays*, p. 22 (1928).
56. *Criterion*, 'Commentary', July 1932.
57. *The Use of Poetry and the Use of Criticism*, pp. 151–3.
58. *A Choice of Kipling's Verse*, 1941, Introduction p. 10.

6

ELIOT'S 'DARK EMBRYO'

The merger of morals and aesthetics

> 'My brain I'll prove the female to my soul,
> My soul the father, and these two beget
> A generation of still breeding thoughts . . .'
>   *Richard II*, V, v.

> 'These are the poems of Eliot
> By the Uranian muse begot;
> A Man their Mother was,
> A Muse their Sire.'
>   EZRA POUND, *Letters* p. 234

T. S. ELIOT appears at the end of a long struggle against the dogmas of poetry and criticism dominant in Victorian England. Pre-Raphaelites, Aesthetes, Georgians, and Imagists before him had battered with a variety of weapons against the literary conservatism which insisted that a poet's true worth was to be tested (in the words of the *Quarterly Review* quoted in Chapter 4) by 'what he means as a thinker'; and against the conservatism of a public which, applying this test, gave its attention and approval only to those poets who echoed popular feeling. This wall of conservatism was broken finally by war and depression (though the same bricks were to be stacked in a new formation by some of the socialist writers of the 'thirties).

For Eliot, as for Yeats, a poem is to be tested not by what it *says* but by what it *is*. In the literary context traced in the last three chapters the virtue of the Georgian poem was that it 'said' very little; of the Imagist poem that it 'said' nothing: the poem could be ignored, but the wrong test could scarcely be applied.

Similarly, on a higher level of achievement, our judgement that 'Easter 1916' is a fine poem is not reached by measuring a paraphrase of its 'meaning' against our knowledge of the merits of the English, or of the Irish, cause; the poem, being an 'Image' rather than a statement, inhibits an evaluation of this kind and thus effectively distinguishes itself from ordinary discourse.

With the establishment of Eliot as a major critic and poet, 'Truth' was out as a simple test of poetic merit; so was 'Beauty'. The question of what remains as a test of better and worse can be answered in Eliot's case only by a study of his criticism.

A close scrutiny of Eliot's criticism will show, I believe, something which few commentaries on his work have so far considered. It will show the gradual realization of a poetic technique, dependent largely upon moments of 'Inspiration', and designed to bring into balance the two halves of the divided sensibility: a technique which weighs, on the one hand, that part of the poet's mind which rationalizes, constructs, and, in the rhetorician, illegitimately persuades and pleases at the expense of complex truth; and, on the other hand, that passive part of the mind which, independent of the will, negatively comprehends complexity, and provides images to embody it, but fails on its own to construct, assert, or even affirm. Eliot, like Yeats, has been concerned to achieve something more positive than the aesthete's 'Beauty'; and less deceptive than the rhetorician's 'Truth'. And he has found his way towards it by means of a developing critical theory and poetic practice which give equal weight to a 'structure' provided by the positive rational will, and a 'texture' which is the gift of the negative imagination.

It must be said first that Eliot *always* gives equal weight to that quality in the poem—its texture—which arrives independent of the will; and, indeed, that in most of his poetry and criticism he gives more weight to this than to the rational structure. For Eliot, as for Shakespeare's Richard II, the 'brain' is 'female to the soul'. This point must be stressed, because the formidable quality of Eliot's criticism has led many to the mistaken view that he is a coldly deliberate poet, consciously manipulating words for a purpose designed before the writing commenced. Such a view of Eliot is incorrect, and the reason should be obvious enough; for it is the poet of powerful intellect who needs most conscientiously to look for ways of suspending that intellect where its literal preoccupations may ride over the more delicate operations of the imagination. Hence Eliot's recurrent concern with a negative state of mind—a state of 'negative capability' or 'Inspiration'. Since this concern has gone largely unobserved, its existence requires some demonstration before conclusions may be drawn from it.

Three essays written in 1919—'Tradition and the Individual Talent', 'Hamlet', and 'Ben Jonson'—indicate that Eliot in that year was wrestling with the problem of conscious direction and unconscious process in the writing of poetry. The first-named essay, though a rather confused piece of writing, has been perhaps most influential; but its real subject has, I think, been largely ignored. Few critics in the 'twenties and 'thirties paused to sort out the meanings given by their context in this essay to the words 'emotion' and 'feelings'. Eliot's insistence on 'impersonality' and 'tradition' were taken out and waved like banners. This was the new classicism!

It should be made clear then, first, that the poet's escape from 'personality' which Eliot describes in this essay is not an escape from the self, but an escape *further into* the self. The concern of the essay is, in fact, that desire already observed in Yeats to release the poet from his own rational will:

'. . . the mind of the mature poet differs from that of the immature one not precisely in any valuation of "personality", not being necessarily more interesting, or having "more to say", but rather by being a more finely perfected medium in which special, or very varied, feelings are at liberty to enter into new combinations.'[1]

So, the essay continues, when Dante writes Canto XV of the *Inferno*, there is an 'emotion evident in the situation', an emotion which attaches itself naturally to the events there described. But it is not this emotion, common to all human beings confronted with like situations, that turns Dante's account to poetry. The quality which is peculiarly 'poetic' is something arriving automatically, independent of the poet's will, and finding its place in the poem's 'complexity of detail', in particular 'phrases' and 'images'. This 'detail' is thrust up from below the levels of consciousness. For example:

'The last quatrain gives an image, a feeling attaching to an image, which "came", which did not develop simply out of what precedes, but which was probably in suspension in the poet's mind . . . (p. 18).'

'Emotion' as Eliot uses it here, is of the 'personality', the surface mind: the particular 'emotion' behind a work gives that work its own consistency, its own structure. There is an emotion inherent in the events of a play, or equally, one assumes, in the 'ideas' of a poem like Pope's *Essay on Man*. But it is not this 'structural emotion' (p. 20) which makes the poetry:

'. . . the whole effect, the dominant tone, is due to the fact that a number of floating feelings, having an affinity to this emotion by no means superficially evident, have combined with it . . .'[a]

Thus, though the writing of poetry is nothing so simple as 'automatic writing', though the conscious mind must edit what is offered from below the level of consciousness, Eliot sees the process as 'a concentration which does not happen consciously or of deliberation' (p. 21). It is, in fact, a state of negative capability, 'a passive attending upon the event' (p. 21).

In his essay on Jonson, Eliot discusses a poet clearly different from himself, whose work seems all structure, without texture. Jonson does not, as Shakespeare does, 'offer poetry in detail as well as in design'.

'. . . unconscious does not respond to unconscious; no swarms of inarticulate feelings are aroused. The immediate appeal of Jonson is to the mind; his emotional tone is not in the single verse, but in the design of the whole' (p. 148)

It will be noted that however difficult these essays may seem on a first close reading, Eliot is using his terms consistently. They may be arranged in this way:

a Eliot's distinction here of 'structural emotion' and 'floating feelings' will be seen in its context to be similar to J. C. Ransom's distinction between 'structure' and 'texture'.

'impersonal' . . .	'personal'
'unconscious' . . . (conscious)	'mind'
'feelings' . . .	'emotions'
'images, phrases' . . .	'structure'
'detail' . . .	'design'

These words recur in varying contexts, but they are set consistently in opposition to one another. Thus, Shakespeare's characters 'are filled in, by much *detail* or many shifting aspects'. This is not so with Jonson, for Jonson was not only 'conscious' in that area of his work which makes 'every creator . . . also a critic'; 'he was *also conscious in his creations*' (p. 152, italics mine). Here 'detail' at the bottom of one list is opposed to 'conscious' at the top of the other.

Jonson's poetry is described by Eliot as poetry 'of the surface'.

'If we look at the work of Jonson's great contemporaries, Shakespeare, and also Donne and Webster and Tourneur (and sometimes Middleton), have a depth, a third dimension . . . which Jonson's work has not. Their words have often a network of tentacular roots reaching down to the deepest terrors and desires. Jonson's most certainly have not. . . .' (p. 155)

The sources of Shakespeare's art are 'deeper' (the word recurs), more 'complex', more 'obscure'. It is clear that Eliot sees the work of art, distinct from the mere thesis, as something which has drawn up life from 'far below the conscious levels of thought'.[a] Jonson's 'words' do not draw upon this source; yet Eliot believes him to be a considerable poet, something more than a satirist of manners. Thus

'. . . if we dig *beneath* the theory, *beneath* the observation, *beneath* the deliberate drawing and the theatrical and dramatic

a *The Use of Poetry*, p. 119. This last quotation refers to what Eliot calls the 'auditory imagination'; but this auditory imagination is part of the distinctive 'poetic' texture, since 'a poem may tend to realize itself first as a particular rhythm before it reaches expression in words, and . . . this rhythm may bring to birth the idea and the image'. *The Music of Poetry*, University of Glasgow Publications, LVII, 1942, p. 28.

elaboration, there is discovered a kind of power, animating
Volpone . . . which *comes from below the intellect*, and for which
no theory of humours will account.' (p. 157, italics mine)

It has taken some effort on Eliot's part to fit Jonson to his own
conception of a poet. Jonson's satire is dismissed as 'incidental'.
It is acknowledged that he is not a poet in 'detail', in his separate
images. But Eliot finds in the over-all 'design' of a play like
Volpone, one great single image which has its roots 'below the
intellect', and it is this which allows Jonson the title of poet.

The remarks preliminary to Eliot's essay on *Hamlet* are
interesting. *Hamlet* is a dangerous subject for 'the critic with a
mind which is naturally of the creative order'.

'. . . Goethe . . . made of Hamlet a Werther. . . . Coleridge . . .
made of Hamlet a Coleridge; and probably neither of these men
in writing about Hamlet remembered that his first business was
to study a work of art.'[2]

To this we may add that Eliot made of the author of Hamlet an
Eliot. Eliot's preoccupation with the below-conscious sources of
poetry is again evident here. The terms already outlined are
again deployed, and in the same relation one to another, but for
'design', 'structure' or 'structural emotion', 'objective correlative' is now substituted:

'The only way of expressing emotion in the form of art is by
finding an "objective correlative"; in other words, a set of
objects, a situation, a chain of events which shall be the formula
of that *particular* emotion; such that when the external facts,
which must terminate in sensory experience, are given, the
emotion is immediately evoked.' (p. 145)

Into this 'objective correlative' the 'floating feelings' are drawn
from 'below the intellect'. And Shakespeare's problem in
writing *Hamlet* was, as Eliot sees it, that his 'correlative', or
simply his plot, was insufficient to absorb the 'intense feeling'
which rose to fill it.

'*Hamlet*, like the sonnets, is full of some stuff that the writer
could not drag to light, contemplate, or manipulate into art. . . .

And the supposed identity of Hamlet with his author is genuine
to this point: that Hamlet's bafflement at the absence of *objective
equivalent* to his *feelings* is a prolongation of the bafflement of
his creator . . .' (pp. 144–5, italics mine)

Texture, then, has overflowed structure; and Shakespeare is
powerless to inhibit the flow of this 'intense feeling' into the
mould which will not contain it—much as, in Baudelaire's
poetry, 'the content of feeling is constantly bursting the receptacle'.[3]

These three essays—apparently about tradition, Jonson, and
Hamlet respectively—show how obsessively concerned Eliot was
at this time with a process of poetry in which the conscious will
played only the minor role of sub-editor.[a] His remarks imply
a kind of poetic composition at least as dependent on spontaneous 'imagination' and 'inspiration' as that which any of the
romantic poets might have affirmed. This is not, of course, all
there is to be said about Eliot's methods of composition; and I
shall try to fill out the picture in the course of this chapter and
the next. At the moment, however, it is important to have
established two points: first, that Eliot's 'escape from personality' is an escape from 'opinion' and 'rhetoric' which he, in
common with Yeats, felt had marred the poetry written in the
mid-nineteenth century; second, that the 'escape' is made, not
away from the self, but deeper into the self, 'below the levels of
consciousness'.

Once the second of these points is understood it is not surprising to find Eliot, reviewing Ezra Pound in 1919, complaining

a It may be objected that Eliot has written things which seem to
contradict what I have said. For example: 'There is a tendency, and
I think it is a whiggery tendency, to decry this critical toil of the artist;
to propound the thesis that the great artist is an unconscious artist. . . .'
('The Function of Criticism', 1923, *Selected Essays*, p. 30.) My answer
to this is, first, that I am not responsible for Eliot's self-contradictions;
second, that where there are contradictions I have concentrated on
those remarks which seem most honestly to proceed from Eliot's
experience as an artist; and third, that in this particular case the contradiction is more apparent than real, since the artist's 'conscious' task
is seen here as a *critical* editing of what the 'creative' moment has
thrown up.

that some of the poems fail to achieve impersonality because
they were not written with sufficient spontaneity:

'The two poems mentioned irritate; *they make you conscious
of having been written by somebody; they have not written themselves.* There are lines in them which are too much the voice of
the accidental human being with a smile in conversation.'[4]

The ground Eliot holds in common with the romantics
follows, perhaps, from his having inherited that 'aesthetic' mode
which runs from Coleridge and Keats through the pre-Raphaelites, Wilde, and Yeats; or perhaps from his having inherited a
similar mode from the poets of nineteenth-century France.
Eliot rejects what Wilde and Yeats reject: the prophetic strain,
which also runs out of the great Romantics (particularly from
Blake, Wordsworth, and Shelley) and degenerates through the
nineteenth century to touch its nadir in poets like Alfred Austin,
William Watson, and Henry Newbolt. What had been in Blake,
or in Wordsworth, the propounding of a vital philosophy, an
intensely felt view of the human condition, became, in Tennyson
for example, 'descriptions of the moral law for the sake of the
moral law',[5] a mere 'decoration of a morality in vogue'.[6]

Yeats in his maturity returned to a position comparable with
that of Blake, in the sense that his poetry seems to have behind
it a 'philosophy'; but Yeats prevents any simple test of his poems
according to what they 'mean' by the assumption of a series of
dramatic masks. Eliot is more radical even than Yeats in his
refusal to consider poetry as a discursive medium. He insists, for
example, that the activities of poet and philosopher are 'better
performed inside two skulls than one',[7] that 'neither Shakespeare
nor Dante did any real thinking—that was not their job'.[8]

Yet Eliot came with astonishing dexterity and quickness to
perceive what Wilde never, and Yeats in his criticism only slowly,
perceived: that the refusal to accept the moralist's role which
the Victorians imposed on their poets *need not imply a rejection
of all commerce between morals and literature.* Popular morals
are generalized statements which have no place in literature;
urgent, argumentative morals compel the poet to debase his
work to rhetoric. But a true mimesis, a faithful reflection of
experience, implies subtle distinctions between particulars which

need never be forced, but simply exist in the work. The aesthetic concern, in short, could be elevated to a *higher kind of morals*. This, I believe, is Eliot's particular achievement. So we find him writing as early as 1922:

'The character of the serious stage, when he is not simply an ordinary person, is confected of abstract qualities, as loyalty, greed, and so on, to which we are supposed to respond with the proper abstract emotions. But the myth is not composed of abstract qualities; it is a point of view, transmuted to importance; it is made by the transformation of the actual by the imaginative genius.

'The modern dramatist, and probably the modern audience, is terrified of the myth. The myth is imagination and it is also criticism, and the two are one. The seventeenth century had its own machinery of virtues and vices, as we have, *but its drama is a criticism of humanity far more serious than its conscious moral judgements*.'[9]

The most profound moral quality of literature does not proceed from the author's '*conscious* moral judgements', for these judgements are of the surface mind, of the 'personality'. Yet 'all first rate poetry is occupied with morality'.[10] How, then, is the poet to achieve this moral quality? Eliot's answer is quite simple: by a total conscious preoccupation with *technique*.

'Is anyone seriously interested in Milton's view of good and evil? Tennyson *decorated the morality he found in vogue*. . . . As for the present time, the *lack of curiosity in technical matters* of the academic poets of today (Georgians et caetera) *is only an indication of their lack of curiosity in moral matters*.'[11]

The question which naturally follows is this: how does a poet's concern with 'technique' achieve a more profound moral view than a conscious concern with morals? The answer, I think, can be found in Eliot's concern with Tradition, and later with Orthodoxy.

In 'The Function of Criticism' Eliot reaffirms the necessity for a living relationship between the artist and the Tradition. On to this concern for tradition Eliot grafts his belief that the poet must not be conscious of a *purpose* in the writing of a poem.

'I do not deny that art may be affirmed to serve ends beyond itself; *but art is not required to be aware of these ends*, and indeed performs its function, whatever that may be, according to various theories of value, much better by indifference to them.'[12]

The poet, conscious of a moral purpose, will 'decorate the morality he [finds] in vogue', as Tennyson did. Or, alternatively, if he '[approaches] everything with a mind unclouded by current opinions', as Blake did, consciousness of a moral purpose will cause him to construct his own 'philosophy', 'an ingenious piece of home-made furniture'.[13]

'What [Blake's] genius required, and what it sadly lacked, was a framework of accepted and traditional ideas which would have prevented him from indulging in a philosophy of his own, and concentrated his attention upon the problems of the poet.'

'The problems of the poet' are technical problems. His conscious mind should be busy at its sub-editor's desk, sorting, abridging, arranging. The moral quality of the work will look after itself—but only if the sensibility of the poet has been thoroughly immersed in the Tradition. 'We are not concerned with the author's *beliefs*', Eliot declares in *After Strange Gods*, '*but with the orthodoxy of sensibility and with the sense of tradition* . . .'[14]. Tradition, or as it later becomes, Orthodoxy, is the background, 'the accumulated wisdom of time'[15] and of the civilization, against which the poet's subconsciously conceived images of 'things as they are' will naturally dispose themselves. The disposition of these images may surprise the poet himself, for as a conscious, responsible citizen, he may be passionately concerned with some current argument about, say, sexual morality, or usury, or politics. But the preoccupation with technique will free him from 'opinion', from the contentiousness of everyday life; it will eliminate the accidental in favour of what is permanent; and the discipline his soul has learned in the school of Tradition will ensure a more lasting image, and a more accurate evaluation, of his subject-matter:

> 'Now shall I make my soul,
> Compelling it to study
> In a learned school
> Till the wreck of body,
> Slow decay of blood,
> Testy delirium
> Or dull decrepitude,
> Or what worse evil come—
> The death of friends, or death
> Of every brilliant eye
> That made a catch in the breath—
> Seem but the clouds of the sky
> When the horizon fades;
> Or a bird's sleepy cry
> Among the deepening shades.'

(W. B. YEATS, 'The Tower')

It should by now be clear that the presence of an 'inspirational' or 'automatic' theory of composition implicit in Eliot's criticism need not seriously clash with the common view of him, the view he himself encouraged: a man of severe intellectual discipline, committed to religious and moral orthodoxy. Eliot did not, of course, initiate a new 'classicism'. He has been 'anti-Romantic' in one sense only: in his refusal to assume, in any form, the mantle of the prophet. Such a refusal does not constitute 'classicism', and there is much ground Eliot holds in common with the Romantics. It remains yet to establish more clearly that this 'inspirational' technique is central to his work as a poet.

A sentence in a short critical note written in 1933,[16] indicates that at this time Eliot was again considering the nature of poetic composition, and that his own experience since 1919 had not changed his earlier view.

'It is the poet's business to be original, in all that is comprehended by "technique", only so far as is absolutely necessary for saying what he has to say; only so far as is dictated, not by the idea—for there is no idea—but by the nature of that dark embryo within him which gradually takes on the form and speech of a poem.'

This image of the writing of poetry as a birth in which the role of the conscious mind is that of midwife, will be seen to recur in Eliot's later critical writings. It is confirmed, though the same image precisely is not employed, in the last of his Charles Eliot Norton lectures of the same year.[17] All good poetry, we may conclude from this lecture, contains much that is strange even to its author. Its imagery draws on memories which 'may have symbolic value, but of what we cannot tell, for they come to represent the depths of feeling into which we cannot peer' (p. 148). The poet himself is unsure of their sources and their meanings. Even where a high degree of organization is necessary —as in a play by Shakespeare—the imagery ('floating feelings') which rises to fill the mould is composed of material which must remain obscure to the author:

'. . . again and again the right imagery, saturated while it lay in the depths of Shakespeare's memory, will rise like Anadyomene from the sea.' (p. 146)

Further, there are times when this efflux comes without any conscious direction, and takes the form of a poem.

'That there is an analogy between mystical experience and some of the ways in which poetry is written I do not deny . . . I know, for instance, that some forms of ill-health, debility or anaemia, may (if other circumstances are favourable) produce an efflux of poetry in a way approaching the condition of automatic writing . . .' (p. 144)

Eliot quotes at this point ('in confirmation of my own experience') a statement by A. E. Housman that 'the production of poetry . . . is less an active than a *passive and involuntary process*' (italics mine, C. K. S.), and that this 'morbid secretion' occurs more readily in a state of debility than in health. To this quotation Eliot appends the remark:

'I take added satisfaction in the fact that I only read Mr Housman's essay some time after my own lines were written.'

He is, in short, pleased to have his own experience confirmed, even by a 'romantic'.

In his introduction to Pascal's *Pensées*,[18] Eliot makes the same point, that ill-health can be conducive to the writing of poetry:

'We know quite well that [Pascal] was at the time when he received his illumination from God in extremely poor health; but it is a common-place that some forms of illness are extremely favourable, not only to religious illumination, but to artistic and literary composition. A piece of writing meditated, apparently without progress, for months or years, may suddenly take shape and word; and in this state long passages may be produced which require little or no re-touch. . . . he to whom this happens assuredly has the sensation of being a vehicle rather than a maker.'

Eliot is careful to distinguish in these passages between the process he is describing and what is commonly known as 'automatic writing'. Yet the processes are markedly similar. How is the distinction made? Only, Eliot explains, by the fact that in the former case 'the material has obviously been incubating within the poet' for a long period:

'. . . it gives the impression, as I have just said, of having undergone a long incubation, though we do not know until the shell breaks what kind of egg we have been sitting on.'[19]

The poet cannot, at the time of composition, will that a duck's egg should produce a cygnet; the quality of the 'dark embryo' has been established by what the poet has made of himself, and what his society has made of him:

'At the moment when one writes, one is what one is, and the damage of a lifetime . . . cannot be repaired at the moment of composition.'[20]

Hence the importance of Eliot's other concern: the saturation of the poet's sensibility in the vats of tradition and orthodoxy ensures a healthy 'embryo' and a healthy poem—something which no effort of the will can achieve.

A consequence of this view of poetry—and one which may now be seen as more responsible than might appear at first glance—is that the 'meaning' of a poem is frequently of secondary importance. It may be there simply 'to satisfy one habit of the reader, to keep his mind diverted and quiet, while the poem does its work upon him'.[21] Meaning is of the poet's conscious will, and it calls to the will of the reader. It is not desirable that the poet should be too precisely concerned with 'meaning', for to prepare it in advance may be to prepare a vessel which will not contain the unknown 'efflux' that arrives to fill it. The 'meaning' of a poem of the kind which interests Eliot can never be predicted before it is written: the structure that awaits the efflux must be flexible. If 'unconscious' is to 'call to unconscious' (as it does not in the particularities of Jonson's verse) the poet is better preoccupied with technical matters than with an exact understanding of what he is about to say. These 'technical exactions' are 'enough to keep the poet's *conscious* mind fully occupied, as the painter's by the manipulation of his tools'.[22]

The relevance of this method of composition to the general theme of this book should by now be clear. The concern with the total 'being' of a poem rather than with its 'meaning' is a way of avoiding the 'dialetical milieu' (see Chapter 5, p. 108), of avoiding the situation in which the poet, too keenly aware of his audience and of its attitude to his subject-matter, adjusts his view of the world either to please or to shock that audience. Eliot has been more absolute even than Yeats in refusing to enter this dialectical relationship between the poet and his audience. More will be said about this refusal, and its effects on Eliot's poetry, in the next chapter. First, however, some more recent critical statements require attention in order to establish the basic consistency and continuity of Eliot's theory.

The writing of an essay on Kipling in 1941[23] was for Eliot a problem similar in kind to the problem of writing on Jonson in 1919. Kipling's poetry is—if it is possible to distinguish between such degrees of unlikeness—even less like Eliot's poetry than

Jonson's is; but it is the same kind of unlikeness. Even more than Jonson's poetry, Kipling's seems all 'structure', all 'conscious'; designed, not to *be*, but to *act*. Once again, as in the essay on Jonson, Eliot feels that there is a quality in Kipling which now and then transcends the 'verse', the deliberate product, and achieves 'poetry'. And again this quality is something which 'breaks through from a deeper level'. Of 'Recessional', for example, Eliot says:

'. . . it is one of those poems in which something breaks through from a deeper level than that of the mind of the conscious observer of political and social affairs. . . .' (p. 16)

But Eliot is even less successful than he was in the Jonson essay in his attempt to establish the presence of this quality. He fails to isolate it, and does not pretend that it occurs more than fitfully. The final effect of his essay is not to establish a new category of poetry which will include Kipling, but to make clearer, and reaffirm, a distinction between 'poetry' which is of the spontaneous imagination, and 'verse' which is of the will; and thus to deny Kipling any substantial footing in the world of poetry. After a considerable struggle with himself, and with Kipling, Eliot only finds it possible to insist that Kipling was a writer of 'great verse', and to remind us of the rareness of the gift for this kind of writing.

Eliot is careful first to acknowledge the difference between himself and Kipling:

'I confess . . . that introspection into my own processes affords no assistance—part of the fascination of this subject is in the explanation of a mind so different from one's own.' (p. 17)

One major difference is that for Kipling poems are 'instruments' to serve a deliberate purpose. His only concern is to find the form which will serve that purpose. The poet (Eliot), on the other hand, tries to find in each new poem 'the right form for feelings over the development of which he has, *as a poet*, no control' (p. 17, italics mine). Here the phrase 'as a poet' implies again 'the damage of a lifetime' which, Eliot tells us in *After*

Strange Gods (see above), 'cannot be repaired at the moment of composition'. The poet *as a man* may condition these feelings by a right attitude to 'tradition' and 'orthodoxy' over a long period—but with such, a versifier like Kipling is not concerned.

One passage in particular in the essay makes clear the distinction between the writer of 'poetry' and the writer of 'verse', and at the same time reveals the consistency of Eliot's thinking on the subject of conscious direction and unconscious process in the writing of poetry:

'I know of no writer of such great gifts for whom poetry seems to have been more purely an instrument. Most of us are interested in the form for its own sake—not apart from the content, but because we aim at making something which shall first of all *be*, something which in consequence will have the capability of exciting, within a limited range, a considerable variety of responses from different readers. For Kipling the poem is something which is intended to *act*—and for the most part his poems are intended to elicit the same response from all readers, and only the response which they can make in common. For other poets—at least for some other poets—the poem may begin to shape itself in fragments of musical rhythm, and its structure will first appear in terms of something analogous to musical form; and such poets find it expedient to occupy their conscious mind with the craftsman's problems, leaving the deeper meaning to emerge from a lower level.' (p. 18)

The implications of these sentences should by now be clear. The conscious mind of the poet occupies itself with 'craftsman's problems' in order to avoid the contentious surface of life, and in order to give his poem, something more than a 'meaning', a *being*. Kipling, on the other hand, remains on that contentious surface, designing each poem to *act* there as an instrument. 'Kipling certainly thought of verse as well as prose as a medium for a public purpose' (p. 26). In this, Eliot adds, Kipling is like Dryden; 'for both, *wisdom has the primacy over inspiration*' (p. 26, italics mine). Clearly Eliot implies that in his own case the proposition is in reverse; and that in all that is essentially poetic, 'inspiration' has the primacy over 'wisdom' (individual, conscious thought).

As in 'The Music of Poetry', so in this essay on Kipling it is argued that the poet's unrealized 'feelings' (which come from below the levels of conscious thought, and which constitute the 'inspiration' of the poem) take their form first in 'fragments of musical rhythm'. Thus

'What fundamentally differentiates his [Kipling's] "verse" from "poetry" is the subordination of musical interest. Many of [Kipling's] poems give, indeed, judged by the ear, an impression of the mood, some are distinctly onomatopoeic: but there is a harmonics of poetry which is not merely beyond their range— *it would interfere with the intention.* . . . from this point of view more "poetry" *would interfere with his purpose.*' (p. 35, italics mine)

Again, I think the proposition may be reversed. A too conscious 'intention' would, from Eliot's point of view, interfere with 'poetry'.

'Verse', then, is of the conscious mind. In 'poetry' the conscious mind is necessary only in order that what is primarily 'poetic' shall have a receptacle into which it may flow.

'. . . the poet who could not write "verse" when verse was needed, would be without that sense of *structure* which is required to make a poem of any length readable.' (p. 36, italics mine)

But what is essentially 'poetic' is not, for Eliot, *of* the conscious mind.

One further essay—a recent one—describes, more vividly than anything else Eliot has written, the intensity of the 'inspirational' process under discussion. Eliot's opening remarks in his 1953 lecture to the National Book League[24] make it clear that he regards his subject as a matter of some importance. Certainly he does not succeed in his attempt 'to avoid saying anything that I have said before' (p. 3). If he *had* succeeded in this, the lecture would be less interesting than it is. What he does achieve is a clearer and simpler statement of a theory he has struggled many times to express in his prose.

The distinctions Eliot makes between his 'Three Voices of Poetry' are, at first glance, simple ones:

'[The first voice is that] of the poet talking to himself—or to nobody. The second is the voice of the poet addressing an audience, whether large or small. The third is the voice of the poet when he attempts to create a dramatic character speaking in verse. . . .' (p. 4)

For examples from his own work of the third voice, Eliot refers, of course, to his plays. His choruses to *The Rock* are cited as examples of the second voice—'that of myself addressing —indeed haranguing—an audience' (p. 7). Eliot makes no reference to examples of the first voice in his own work, but it is clear from what follows that he considers his major poetry to be predominantly (though not entirely, for such a thing would be impossible) of the first voice. Poetry of the second voice 'has a conscious social purpose', and it is already clear that Eliot rejects such a purpose, is one of those poets who 'find it expedient to occupy their conscious mind with craftsman's problems'.[25] Kipling's poetry—or 'verse'—is almost entirely of the second voice; so is Dryden's. And Eliot has already acknowledged his difference from poets of this kind.

How, then, for the poet of the first voice—'that which is not primarily an attempt to communicate with anyone at all'[26]—does the experience of writing poetry feel?

'. . . the German poet Gottfried Benn, in a very interesting lecture entitled *Probleme der Lyrik*, thinks of lyric as the poetry of the first voice: he includes, I feel sure, such poems as Rilke's Duino Elegies and Valéry's *La Jeune Parque*. . . .

'What, asks Herr Benn in this lecture, does the writer of such a poem "addressed to no-one", start with? There is, first, he says, an inert embryo or "creative germ" (*ein dumpfer schöpferischer Keim*), and, on the other hand, the Language, the resources of the words at the poet's command. He has something germinating in him for which he must find words; but he cannot know what words he wants until he has found the words; he cannot identify this embryo until it has been transformed into an arrangement of the right words in the right order. When you have the words for it, the "thing" for which the words had to be found has disappeared, replaced by a poem. What you start from is *nothing so definite as an emotion*, in any ordinary sense; *it is still more certainly not an idea*; it is—to adapt two lines of Beddoes to a different meaning—a

> bodiless childful of life in the gloom
> Crying with frog-voice, "what shall I be?"

I agree with Gottfried Benn, and I would go a little further. In a poem which is neither didactic nor narrative, and not animated by any other social purpose, the poet may be concerned solely with expressing in verse—using all his resources of words, with their history, their connotations, their music—this obscure impulse. *He does not know what he has to say until he has said it.* . . . He is oppressed by a burden which he must bring to birth in order to obtain relief. Or, to change the figure of speech, he is haunted by a demon, a demon against which he feels power-less, because in its first manifestation it has no face, no name, nothing: and the words, the poem he makes, are a kind of . . . exorcism of this demon. In other words again, he is going to all that trouble, not in order to communicate with anyone, but to gain relief from acute discomfort; and when the words are finally arranged in the right way—or in what he comes to accept as the best arrangement he can find—he may experience a moment of exhaustion, of appeasement, of absolution, and of something very near annihilation, which is in itself indescribable.' (p. 17–18, italics mine)

This is the most intense and the most personal statement Eliot has made about the processes of composition. And it is important to note that the poetry of the first voice is described as 'a more *impersonal* voice still than that of either the character or the author' (p. 21, italics mine). Here, I think, is confirmation of the interpretation already placed in this chapter on the term 'impersonality' as it occurs in the early essays. It is a direction inward, not outward, in order to discover what is eternal. The impersonal voice is not what Eliot calls (in 'The Function of Criticism') 'the Inner Voice'; for the Inner Voice is the voice of conscious, individualistic thought—the voice of 'opinion' which belongs to rhetoric and to heresy. The 'impersonal voice' lies deeper. It is the voice of the poet's 'soul'—that part of his being which is unknowable, even to himself. It expresses itself, not in 'thought', but by a recreation of diverse experience into 'feeling' —which in turn becomes ('something rich and strange') the essential texture of the poem.[a]

Of course, not all Eliot's non-dramatic poetry has been composed in the way described above: the first and second voices, Eliot goes on to say, are found side by side in a single poem. And all three voices may be heard at different times in a play. But however necessary the second voice may be in order that the non-dramatic poem may have structural coherence, it is clear that for Eliot the first voice is the voice of *poetry*, the voice that speaks out of the still centre of his own best work. Conversely, just as the first voice may rise now and then to surprise poets like Dryden, Pope, and Byron, it is the second voice, the voice which 'addresses you as if you were a public meeting' that is the staple of their poems.[27] These poets decide, consciously, and in advance of the poem, what form their address shall take.

'. . . the form is already to some extent given. However much it may be *trans*formed before the poem is finished, it can be represented from the start by an outline or scenario.' (p. 22)

In the purest poems of the first voice on the other hand, the feeling itself determines the form:

'. . . the "psychic material" tends to create its own form—the eventual form will be to a greater or less degree the form for that one poem and for no other.' (p. 22)

Eliot's attitude both to his audience and to his 'subject matter' is a direct reaction against critical and creative habits already

---

a The various statements by Eliot on this process are well enough known. They occur, for example, in 'The Metaphysical Poets' (1921) and in 'Philip Massinger' (1920).

observed in Chapters 3 and 4—habits inherited largely from the Victorians. The writer who argued in the *Quarterly Review* in 1908 that 'the ultimate standard by which [a poet's] rank and his significance are to be measured is what he means as a thinker, as an observer, as an impassioned critic of life, not the manner in which he produced his notes as a singer'—this writer would find no satisfaction in Eliot's insistence that *qua* poet he was not a thinker at all, that he could not predict until a poem was written what it might 'say' or 'mean'; and, indeed, that if the poem has a 'meaning' at all, the importance of this 'meaning' is for him (if not for Dryden or for Pope—or, in a different way, for Blake) secondary to the poem's 'being', its existence as a complex and irreducible Image. In Eliot's view, a poem is not moral by saying 'moral' things—as his attitude to Tennyson indicates; and his essay on Baudelaire, or, to take another example, his remarks on Ford's *'Tis Pity She's a Whore*, show that he does not consider a poem is immoral for saying, or describing, 'immoral' things. A poem is 'moral' only in being *complete*, in being healthy, a true mimesis of 'things as they are', a product of the undivided sensibility in tune with 'the Nature of Things'.[28] And such a poem can only be written out of humility —the humility of the man before the Tradition, and of the poet's conscious mind before his limited technical problems.

Similarly any test of a poem in terms of what an articulate audience expects of it is, for Eliot, irrelevant. The poet may choose to adopt the second voice, to address his audience. But we are advised, even in reading poets of this kind, to listen for the moment when the true voice of poetry—the first voice— rises above the second.[29] And when the first voice speaks, the poet *qua* poet is no more concerned with an audience than he is concerned with 'ideas':

'. . . he is not concerned with making people understand any- thing. He is not concerned, at this stage, with other people at all: only with finding the right words, or, anyhow, the least wrong words. He is not concerned whether anybody else will ever listen to them or not, or whether anybody else will ever understand them if he does.' (p. 18)

And when the process of writing is complete

'. . . then he can say to the poem: "Go away! Find a place for yourself in a book—and don't expect *me* to take any further interest in you." '

What the poet wants to make of the subject, and what his audience believes ought to be made of it, are matters too transient and unimportant for the permanence of art. It is 'the octopus or angel with which the poet struggles' (p. 22) that has permanence beyond both poet and audience. In the way already described, the poem must determine itself; and in this self-determination a quality is achieved which merges and transcends both 'morals' and 'aesthetics' as these were separately understood in the criticism of the late nineteenth century. 'Inspiration' as it occurs in Eliot's writing is only correctly understood if it is thought of, not as self-abandonment, but as the most rigorous of all disciplines—the discipline which negates the conscious rational individual man in favour of the 'shaping spirit of imagination'.[30]

REFERENCES

1. *Selected Essays*, 3rd enlarged ed., 1951, p. 18.
2. 'Hamlet', ibid., p. 141.
3. *Selected Essays*, p. 424.
4. *Athenaeum*, 24 October 1919. Italics mine.
5. Yeats, *Ideas of Good and Evil*, p. 320.
6. Eliot, *Tyro*, 1922.
7. *The Use of Poetry* . . . , p. 99.
8. *Selected Essays*, p. 136.
9. 'The Romantic Englishman . . .' *Tyro*, 1922. Italics mine.
10. 'The Lesson of Baudelaire', *Tyro*, 1922.
11. ibid. Italics mine.
12. *Selected Essays*, p. 24. Italics mine.
13. 'William Blake', *Selected Essays*, pp. 320–2.
14. *After Strange Gods*, p. 38. Italics mine.
15. *Selected Essays*, p. 29.
16. *Collected Poems of Harold Monro*, edited by Alida Monro, with a critical note by T. S. Eliot.
17. *The Use of Poetry and the Use of Criticism*, 1933, p. 143.
18. Translated by W. F. Trotter, 1931. See *Selected Essays*, p. 405.
19. *The Use of Poetry* . . . , p. 144.
20. *After Strange Gods*, 1934, p. 26.

21. *The Use of Poetry* . . . , p. 151.

22. ibid., p. 154. Italics Eliot's.

23. *A Choice of Kipling's Verse*, made by T. S. Eliot, with an essay on Rudyard Kipling, 1941.

24. 'The Three Voices of Poetry', Cambridge, 1953.

25. 'Kipling', p. 18—see above.

26. 'The Three Voices . . .', p. 15.

27. ibid., p. 24.

28. See *On Poetry and Poets*, 1957, p. 105.

29. 'The Three Voices . . .', p. 24.

30. Coleridge, *Dejection*.

7

THE POETRY OF T. S. ELIOT
Affirmation and the Image

> 'To be a poet is to have a soul so quick to discern that no
> shade of quality escapes it, and so quick to feel, that
> discernment is but a hand playing with finely-ordered
> variety on the chords of emotion—a soul in which know-
> ledge passes instantaneously into feeling and feeling
> flashes back as a new organ of knowledge. One may have
> that condition by fits only.'
>
> GEORGE ELIOT, *Middlemarch*, Chapter XXII

PERHAPS the most disturbing observation to be made concerning
T. S. Eliot is the degree to which the literary world, since it
found it could not eject his early poetry, has succeeded in digest-
ing, dissolving, assimilating that poetry until it is apt to appear
innocuous—only discourse with a suppression of certain 'links
in the chain' (a phrase for which Eliot was himself unhappily
responsible). The critical process which has done most harm to
'The Waste Land', for example, began with the best of intentions.
The poem was attacked as 'meaningless'; to critics who perceived its merits, such attacks were intolerable. Books and
articles were written 'explaining' Eliot. But no critic concerned
primarily with 'meaning' could touch the true *being* of the early
poetry. It has been the inevitable result of the literary conventions and conservatism described in this book, that so many
of the 'explanations' of Eliot's poetry have only moved in orbit
about their subject, emitting faint signals about its outer atmosphere. It is fifty years since 'The Waste Land' appeared, and in
some ways we are still helpless before it. It is unmistakably

there; but we have evolved no adequate language for discussing it. Parts of the poem stand (this is not a question of 'evaluation') with a few other poems ('Kubla Khan' is another example) as the purest 'poetry' in the language, the irreducible 'first voice'. It is not a vehicle, or an agent, but a self-contained poetic entity. The only way it can be said to 'act' is in offering an experience which modifies and enriches the sensibility of the reader.

'The Waste Land' is, then, the end product of successive movements against abstractable poetic discourse; it is the justification of the Symbolist enterprise, the poem which fulfils Arthur Symons's literary prophecy (quoted as epigraph to this book). It contains, I believe, some of Eliot's finest poetry. It represents also the perfection of a method which perhaps prevents Eliot from achieving the kind of greatness Yeats achieved.

In this chapter I shall try to make these generalizations meaningful.

Eliot's reliance as a poet on the creative moment which occurs independent of the will (see Chapter 6) ought to warn against the assumption that his poems—or at any rate the best of his early poems—follow a structure of 'ideas' or narrative which existed in outline before the poem began. Many of his critics have assumed that such a structure, if it did not exist prior to the poem, at least developed as the poem developed. The assumption is, for example, that Prufrock has a fixed identity, is abstractable from the poem as a delineated character. Thus Mr George Williamson discusses Prufrock's 'psychological block' and his 'great dread of public revelation of himself'.[1] Puzzled by the fact that the voice of the poem addresses someone as 'you' ('here beside you and me'), and yet refers to a lady as 'one' ('If one, settling a pillow beside her head, Should say . . .'), Mr Williamson concludes that the 'you' addressed is also Prufrock: 'you and me' are the two halves of Prufrock's mind. 'One' is the lady before whom Prufrock finds himself incapable of declaring his intentions. If such questions were useful, one would like Mr. Williamson to say which Prufrock takes 'toast and tea', and which takes 'tea and cakes and ices'; and why both seem to have measured out their lives in coffee spoons.

Mr Williamson's assumption is that there is a structure of discourse, that only connecting links have been omitted. 'Reading [Eliot's] poetry,' he argues, 'is essentially like reading that of other poets'.[2] I disagree with this premise, and hence with the method Mr Williamson employs in his readings of the early poetry.

When we read a poem by Yeats, or Tennyson, or Milton, or Spenser, or Chaucer, we perceive at once—whatever else there may be in the poem—a sequence, a temporal (narrative), or spatial (descriptive), or logical structure. 'The Waste Land', on the other hand, is likely to seem poetry aspiring to the condition of music: 'a structure like that of a Bach fugue' (as Yeats says in surprise at Pound's *Cantos*); '. . . no plot, no chronicle of events, no logic of discourse'.[3] This first impression, that we are facing a poetry which is significantly different from most other poetry in the language, is not, I believe, deceptive in the way many of Eliot's critics would have us believe. The structures these critics impose on the poems in order to demonstrate that each has precise 'meaning', are frequently not validated by the poems themselves. My objection is not a general objection to what Mr Cleanth Brooks calls 'the heresy of paraphrase'. Most poetry in English, as Mr Brooks's critical practice shows, lends itself to paraphrase; and so long as the paraphrase is written and read on the understanding that it is *only* paraphrase and can never exhaust the poem, it can do little harm. However inadequate to their subjects, the following statements seem to me, in their limited way, true statements: 'Easter 1916' dramatizes a complex, but single, view of a political event; Pope's 'Essay on Man' expresses certain ideas about the human condition; Marvell's 'To His Coy Mistress' dramatizes the insistent voice of the lover aware of mortality; many of Spenser's poems tell stories. But it seems to me false to say that 'The Love Song of J. Alfred Prufrock' dramatizes the voice of the middle-aged would-be suitor;[a] just as it seems false to say that there is a 'statement of beliefs' in 'The Waste Land' which emerges 'through confusion and cynicism, not in spite of them'.[4] We are dealing with poetry of a kind which resists the terms in which we are accustomed to speak of our experience as readers. Professor L. C. Knights has said:

'. . . there are passages in Shakespeare (as indeed in other poets) where even this tentative and exploratory procedure [paraphrase] is of a very limited usefulness indeed, for what we

[a] F. O. Matthiessen refers to 'the middle-aged Prufrock'. *The Achievement of T. S. Eliot*, p. 58.

are given is not the poetic apprehension of thought, but thought in the process of formation. Such a passage is the speech of Macbeth in the moment of temptation ("This supernatural soliciting cannot be ill; cannot be good . . .") where we are directly aware both of the emotional and the bodily accompaniments of a state of being issuing in a conception that will not easily yield itself to conceptual forms ("my thought, whose murder yet is but fantastical . . ."). Such again is that other great soliloquy, "If it were done, when 'tis done . . ." where the meaning is composed of an emotional current running full-tilt against an attempted logical control. In the *Hamlet* passage ["To be or not to be . . ."] the pace is more meditative, but such ideas as it contains are held loosely in relation to a current of feeling which is the main determinant of meaning.'[5]

Professor Knights's account of these moments in Shakespeare's poetry in which the intensity and depth of feeling radically modifies, or may even render unimportant, whatever 'meaning' the poetry has as statement, points at least *towards* the kind of definition which seems to me applicable to the best of Eliot's early poetry. 'The Waste Land' is composed of a series of projections of 'states of feeling', having no fixed centre but their common origin in the depths of one man's mind. The poem traces in its rhythms, in its music, and in the sequence of its images, the events of that mind at a particular time and in relation to a particular set of external circumstances—circumstances of which we can only ever know a very little. Neither a reading of *From Ritual to Romance*, nor visits to Lausanne and Margate, will help us towards a more complete experience of the poem. Eliot's intellectual and physical experiences—the books he read, the places he visited—are employed in various ways as vehicles for his feeling. But it is the feeling, not the experience, which is the poem's 'subject'.

If one contemplates 'The Waste Land' long enough it can seem the most uncompromising poetry ever written in English, wrung, like 'Kubla Khan', from a mind so confident in abstract discourse, so capable of 'explaining' itself, that the procession of non-discursive images could only have been achieved by a discipline amounting to self-annihilation. What opium or some rarely attained dream state precipitated in Coleridge in 1797 (*pace* Miss Elisabeth Schneider), a 'breakdown' precipitated more thoroughly in Eliot in the winter of 1921.[a] In each case we face a kind of poetry that has seldom appeared in our literature— a pure, non-discursive Image—and we must speak about it accordingly.

'The Love Song of J. Alfred Prufrock' is a poem composed of a number of sections put together in a manner which looks forward to the 'The Waste Land'. Sections are rearranged, lines put in, others taken out: yet the poem does not suffer, for its coherence depends on consistency of feeling, not on a fixed sequence of idea or event. Some of the lines were composed in Harvard, some in Paris, some in Germany; and as Hugh Kenner has said, the poem 'bears traces of its prolonged incubation'.[6]

In the first twelve lines a voice invites us (or someone) to follow it through a dream-wilderness of 'half-deserted streets'. Then comes the isolated couplet

> 'In the room the women come and go
> Talking of Michelangelo.'

—'meaningless', but, in some peculiar way, resonant in its context. It does not occur to us to ask *where* this room is, in what relation it stands to the streets of the preceding lines. The poem is a representation, not of the visible world, but of a state of mind.

In the next section—lines 15 to 22—there is a change from direct speech to orthodox past tense description. But again we scarcely feel the change. We do not ask *when* the yellow fog 'licked its tongue into the corners of the evening'; whether this happened before or after the voice invited us to follow it. Normal temporal or spacial relationships do not apply, any more than they apply in listening to music.

The mind which is attempting in 'Prufrock' to give substance to its own deep, half-apprehended feelings, is the mind of a young man.[b] It is immature; its store of experience, of 'felt life',

a 'Last winter [Eliot] broke down, and was sent off for three months rest. During that time he wrote *The Waste Land*.' *The Letters of Ezra Pound*, p. 241.

b Mr Hugh Kenner records that Eliot 'once referred casually to Prufrock . . . as a *young man*'. *The Invisible Poet*, p. 40.

is insufficiently rich to maintain the poem's concretion. And there is not yet sufficient certainty in the editing consciousness, of what lines fail to take life. So in lines 23–34 there is a loss of firmness: the attempt to fix a mood slides into vacuous gestures:

> 'And indeed there will be time
> For the yellow fog that slides along the street
> Rubbing its back upon the window panes;
> There will be time, there will be time
> To prepare a face to meet the faces that you meet;
> There will be time to murder and create
> And time for all the works and days of hands
> That lift and drop a question on your plate.'

There is, as Eliot has said, precise and imprecise emotion, just as there is precise and imprecise thought. In these lines precision has been lost.

The couplet is now repeated, bringing again the timeless, placeless room in which the women talk of Michelangelo.

The voice returns, and speaks in the person of a man poised —like a man who faces a closed door at the top of a flight of stairs—before something which his own mind fails to bring into a defining focus. (Here the sense of failure materializes in those Laforguean props—baldness, thinness, morning coat, collar and tie—which have provided critics with descriptive matter for the particularized, ageing Prufrock they have imposed on the poem as a whole.)

The poem continues in this way, following a dream labyrinth of smoke-filled streets, stairways, rooms, which lead only back into the uncertain mind which created the labyrinth as an image of its own vain endeavour to find itself. Here and there the 'fog' disperses and an image forms (though 'image' suggests too sharply a visual quality) of unfulfilled sexual aspiration, and the lethargy that accompanies it:

> 'And I have known the arms already, known them all—
> Arms that are braceleted and white and bare
> (But in the lamplight, downed with light-brown hair!) . . .
> Arms that lie along a table, or wrap about a shawl.'

These lines, as the rhymes indicate, belong together. But the young literary man, the conscious editor fearing self-revelation (or self-discovery), interposes the ironic couplet

> 'Is it perfume from a dress
> Which makes me so digress?'

There is nothing more substantial in the poem than this insistent aspiration, and the lines which express it are hardly 'digressions' from anything else; but these lines are broken up and dispersed through the poem. After a group of five lines, divided off from the rest by rows of dots, the poem's central preoccupation returns:

> 'And the afternoon, the evening, sleeps so peacefully
> Smoothed by long fingers,
> Asleep . . . tired . . . or it malingers,
> Stretched on the floor, here beside you and me.
> Should I, after tea and cakes and ices,
> Have the strength to force the moment to its crisis.'

But the editing consciousness again intervenes, and there is another escape into Laforguean self-mockery:

> 'But though I have wept and fasted, wept and prayed,
> Though I have seen my head, grown slightly bald
>   brought in upon a platter,
> I am no prophet—and here's no great matter;
> I have seen the moment of my greatness flicker,
> And I have seen the eternal Footman hold my coat,
>   and snicker,
> And in short, I was afraid.'

We move on through a series of verbal gestures, their repetitiveness atoned for only by the exactness with which the music of the lines accompanies the mime of meaningful speech—

> 'And would it have been worth it after all,
> Would it have been worth while,
> After the sunsets and the dooryards and the
>   sprinkled streets,

> After the novels, after the teacups, after the
>   skirts that trail along the floor—
> And this, and so much more?—
> It is impossible to say just what I mean!'

—on through this to 'the paragraph about Hamlet . . . an early and cherished bit' which 'T. E. won't give up.'[7] Pound's dislike of the Hamlet passage is easy to understand. It defines in sharp abstractions a Polonius who bears little relation to the shadowy uncertain identity which is the voice of the poem. It is the abstract delineation of a mind, not a living image. The clever young literary man has again taken command.

In the last six lines the living image returns, and seems to contain, latent if not realized, a vision of ecstatic sexual fulfilment, frustrated by the voices of reality. But now we are on the fringes of a new poem—far from streets, stairways, and rooms, lingering 'in the chambers of the sea'.

'Prufrock' is a poem radically different from the common stock of poetry in 1911, the year of composition. Eliot's rejection of discursive poetry is complete. We cannot ask what the poem means, but only what it *is*. And the answer can only be general: it is a poem which attempts to project and universalize a state of mind. To know better what it is, we must enter the poem.

In 1908 Eliot had read of Laforgue's poetry

> 'It is an art of the nerves, this art of Laforgue, and it is what all art would tend towards if we followed our nerves on all their journeys.'[8]

Eliot 'followed his nerves' in Prufrock:

> 'It is impossible to say just what I mean!
> But as if a magic lantern threw the nerves in
>   patterns on a screen.'

and in a number of other poems published in his first volume— 'Portrait of a Lady', 'Preludes', and 'La Figlia Che Piange' being the most notable of them. This period of development ended around 1917 with the agreement between Pound and Eliot that 'the dilution of *vers libre* . . . had gone far enough and that some

counter current must be set going. . . . Remedy prescribed:
Émaux et Camées . . . Rhyme and regular strophes'.[9] The poems
which resulted from this decision are not typical of Eliot's best
work. Most of them are highly conscious, deliberate, frequently
satiric—examples of good verse-making, as Eliot himself defines
verse, rather than poems:

> 'Donne I suppose was such another
> Who found no substitute for sense,
> To seize and clutch and penetrate;
> Expert beyond experience,
>
> 'He knew the anguish of the marrow
> The ague of the skeleton;
> No contact possible to flesh
> Allayed the fever of the bone.'

Two years of effort, however, in this more traditional and deliberate method of composition, and Eliot could use it to command
a considerable range of feeling. It is interesting that Yeats, with
all of Eliot's lyric poetry before *Four Quartets* to choose from,
included three of these quatrain poems in his *Oxford Book of
Modern Verse*, and nothing from 'The Waste Land' or 'Ash
Wednesday'. In his Introduction, Yeats quotes lines from
'Sweeney Among the Nightingales' which, he says, 'speak in the
grand manner':

> 'The host with someone indistinct
> Converses at the door apart,
> The nightingales are singing in
> The convent of the Sacred Heart,
>
> 'And sang within the bloody wood
> When Agamemnon cried aloud,
> And let their liquid siftings fall
> To stain the stiff dishonoured shroud.'

What Yeats sought for and failed to find in Eliot's work—'except
where his remarkable sense of actor, chanter, scene, sweeps him
away'—was 'rhythmical animation'.[10] By means of his dramatic

masks, Yeats had found his way to objectivity, 'impersonality', without loss of affirmative speech. He could hardly be expected to understand, at this point in his own career, that the passive, undriven music of Eliot's best poetry was a more radical progress over the same ground that he (Yeats) had covered in the 'nineties:

> 'Stand on the highest pavement of the stair—
> Lean on a garden urn—
> Weave, weave the sunlight in your hair—
> Clasp your flowers to you with a pained surprise—
> Fling them to the ground and turn
> With a fugitive resentment in your eyes:
> But weave, weave the sunlight in your hair.'

For Yeats in 1935, such thoroughly sensuous poetry as 'La Figlia Che Piange', or even 'The Waste Land'—poetry in which 'texture' was all-important and 'structure' only a shadow— was the art of 'the man helpless before the contents of his own mind'.[11] Contrary to the critical dogmas he had affirmed in his youth, Yeats had come to prefer the affirmative rhythms of the will (expressed, however, through an 'impersonal' mask) to this subtler music of the 'soul'.

In 1919 Eliot's brief period as a conscious manipulator of elegant satiric verse ended with the writing of 'Gerontion'. 'Gerontion', like 'Prufrock', is an expression of something which has its genesis at a deeper level than that of the conscious will— and here, for the first time, the 'psychic material', 'the octopus or angel with which the poet struggles',[12] takes on the dark stain of some intense suffering which carries over into 'The Waste Land'. The gentle youthful aspirations of 'Prufrock' have passed through fulfilment into some unimagined horror in which all desire that issues in action is seen as destructive. In the passionate pursuit of some essential quality—beauty, or truth, or merely 'life' itself—beauty turns to terror and passion destroys itself:

> 'I that was near your heart was removed therefrom
> To lose beauty in terror, terror in inquisition.
> I have lost my passion.'

Whatever is attained in the pursuit, and possessed, loses the quality which encouraged the pursuer—

'Since what is kept must be adulterated.'

The 'house' of which Gerontion speaks seems variously his own (rented) house, turned brothel; his body, the decaying house in which his soul is prostituted; and the body of a woman turned prostitute.

> 'Think at last
> We have not reached conclusion, when I
> Stiffen in a rented house.'

Here 'stiffen', like some Elizabethan puns on 'die', compresses sexual intercourse and death into a single corruption. Again in the lines

> 'And an old man driven by the Trades
> To a sleepy corner'

'Trades' suggests more than the winds which blow incessantly through the poem. The word seems to carry something of the meaning it has in *Measure for Measure*[a] which provides the poem's epigraph:

> 'How would you live, Pompey? by being a bawd?
> What do you think of the trade Pompey? is it
> a lawful trade?'

The wind is an image of time. It is the consciousness of time (History) and hence of death that drives us ('driven by the Trades') towards sexual experience which is another kind of death ('a sleepy corner'). So all who are alive are old like Gerontion, close to death; all 'stiffen in a rented house'. Everything must be borne away on the wind—

> 'Beyond the circuit of the shuddering bear
> In fractured atoms.'

Finally the poem leaves us only the image of the Gull—innocence, imagination, spirit—fighting its battle with time ('against

a Just as 'kept' and 'adulterated' in the line quoted above suggest perhaps the shadowy figure of a 'kept' woman and an 'adulteress'.

the wind'), both raped ('running on the Horn') and seduced ('the Gulf claims'):

> 'Gull against the wind, in the windy straits
> Of Belle Isle, or running on the Horn,
> White feathers in the snow, the Gulf claims,
> And an old man driven by the Trades
> To a sleepy corner.'

Some such feeling as I have outlined here seems to lie behind 'Gerontion', but Eliot, I think, fails to project it into a coherent poem. Only a pattern imposed by a critic willing to do some of the poet's structural work for him will give the poem an appearance of completeness. The mixture of images from Eliot's current reading, together with what seem to be echoes of contemporary events, form a rich and varied condensation of experience which fails in this case to hold together as a coherent poem. 'Gerontion' has been found by various critics to contain echoes from Henry Adams's *Education*, H. C. Benson's *Edward Fitzgerald*, Lancelot Andrews' *Sermons*, Joyce's *Ulysses, Bussy D'Ambois, Measure for Measure,* and *The Changeling*. No doubt there are other sources yet undiscovered. Hugh Kenner[13] suggests further that the 'wilderness of mirrors' and History's 'contrived corridors' have their genesis in news of Versailles and the Polish Corridor. And I add a suggestion: that the phrase 'fractured atoms' would not have occurred to Eliot a year earlier—since it was June 1919, at the time of the Versailles conference, that the first splitting of the atom (by Ernest Rutherford) was announced. More significant, of course, if such source hunting were important, would be phrases which could be found to establish direct links with events in the poet's private life. In 'Gerontion' Eliot fulfils his own description of the poet as a man in whom, by a strange chemical process, 'disparate experiences . . . are always forming new wholes'.[14] But the poem shows, I think, that the sorting out of these private experiences is no aid to our understanding. The concern of criticism is not these experiences, but the emotional unity and depth of the 'new whole'. In 'Gerontion' coherence is not fully achieved.

Eliot perhaps felt this incompleteness himself. The writing of

'Gerontion' seems to have precipitated a number of ideas in his three 1919 essays discussed in Chapter 6, one of which contains the theory of the 'objective correlative'. '*Hamlet*, like the sonnets,' he writes in this essay, 'is full of some stuff the author could not drag to light, contemplate, or manipulate into art.' The 'stuff' which fails to find expressive form is described as 'intense feeling, ecstatic or terrible, without an object or exceeding its object'; and Eliot adds that such a feeling 'is something which every person of sensibility has known'. We may take it, then, that he is speaking of his own experience, and it is likely, I think, that such a feeling as this failed to find a satisfactory 'correlative' in the persona of Gerontion. Eliot's own realization of this failure would account for the attempted self-explanation of the con-cluding lines of the poem—

'Tenants of a house,
Thoughts of a dry brain in a dry season.'

which stand out as an obvious and unsatisfactory attempt to cast order and meaning back over the whole poem.

Another idea which seems likely to have come direct from the writing of 'Gerontion' is that the poet has not a personality to express but only 'a particular medium . . . in which impressions and experiences combine in peculiar and unexpected ways'; and in the same essay[15] an insistence on 'the historical sense', the poet's necessary loss of 'personality' in the presence of the significant past—an idea which bears at least some relation to those lines in 'Gerontion' where Clio and Erato seem to merge into a single Muse:

'Think now
History has many cunning passages, contrived
                              corridors
And issues, deceives with whispering ambitions,
Guides us by vanities. Think now
She gives when our attention is distracted
And what she gives, gives with such supple
                              confusions
That the giving famishes the craving.'

The 'psychic material' which fails to find its 'objective correlative' in 'Gerontion' is brought to a clearer focus in 'The Waste Land'. It is not part of my intention to offer another full discussion of the poem, but only to place it more firmly in the historical context which is the subject of this book; in other words, to establish more clearly what has been asserted already—that 'The Waste Land' is the end-product of a prolonged movement against discursive poetry, and that it cannot be seen accurately if it is read only as discourse from which certain 'links in the chain' have been omitted. Above all, a critic of this poetry must avoid turning Eliot's 'ideas' into a system and then applying the system like a strait-jacket to the poem. We have sufficient warning in Eliot's criticism against such a procedure. The poet's mind is eclectic: it ranges about among various sources, selecting images, translating ideas into images, not in order to arrive at a system of thought, but to give form and life to its deepest feelings.

The comparison which perhaps more than any other has confused discussions of Eliot's poetry, is the comparison with Donne and the Metaphysicals. When F. O. Matthiessen, for example, writes that 'the condensation of form that was demanded both by Donne and the Symbolists *logically* builds its effects upon sharp contrasts',[16] the word 'logically', if it means anything, is being used in two quite different senses at once. The conscious, directing intellect, the sinewy logic, the drive towards a particular point, all present in Donne, are absent in Symbolist poetry; on the other hand, there is no room, within the exacting intellectual structure of a Metaphysical poem, for the Symbolists' repetitive, dream-like music—the style which is brought to perfection in 'The Waste Land'.

Three general statements made by early critics of 'The Waste Land' establish a firm basis for the discussion of all Eliot's major poems before *Four Quartets*. The first of these is by I. A. Richards. It may be that Richards' accuracy in describing 'The Waste Land' resulted in part from the perfect correspondence of that poem with the generalization Richards was at that time attempting to make about *all* poetry. Nevertheless, the following remarks, published only two years after the appearance of 'The Waste Land', remain an accurate description of the poem and a serviceable warning to its critics:

'Mr Eliot's poetry has occasioned an unusual amount of irritated or enthusiastic bewilderment. The bewilderment has several sources. The most formidable is the unobtrusiveness, in some cases the absence, of any coherent intellectual thread upon which the items of the poem are strung. A reader of "Gerontion", of "Preludes", or of "The Waste Land" may, if he will, after repeated readings, introduce such a thread. Another reader after much effort may fail to contrive one. But in either case energy will have been misapplied. For the items are united by the accord, contrast, and interaction of their emotional effects, not by an intellectual scheme that analysis must work out. The value lies in the unified response which this interaction creates in the right reader. The only intellectual activity required takes place in the realization of the separate items. We can, of course, make a "rationalization" of the whole experience, as we can of any experience. If we do, we are adding something which does not belong to the poem.'[a]

The second general statement comes from R. P. Blackmur, who wrote in 1928:

' "The Waste Land" is neither allegory, nor metaphysics in verse, *nor anything else but poetry*.'[17]

In the same article Blackmur spoke of the 'astonishing purity' of the poem, and added:

'The reason Mr Eliot leaves aside English poetry since the Restoration is that its inspiration is impure . . . its emotions not founded on the facts of feeling exclusively.'

a *Principles of Literary Criticism*, pp. 289–90. On p. 130 of *The Use of Poetry* . . . Eliot expresses disapproval of Richards' statement (In *Science and Poetry*) that 'The Waste Land' effects a 'severance between poetry and *all* beliefs'. Eliot's failure to understand what Richards means here seems deliberate obtuseness, especially since we find him writing on p. 151 of the same book that 'meaning' is only something to keep the reader's mind diverted and quiet while the poem does its work on him. Eliot also seems to have forgotten his own dictum (in 'Shakespeare and the Stoicism of Seneca') that the poet *qua* poet does not believe or disbelieve anything.

And third, F. R. Leavis writing in 1932:

'. . . the unity of "The Waste Land" is no more "metaphysical"
than it is narrative or dramatic, and to try to elucidate it meta-
physically reveals complete misunderstanding. The unity the
poem aims at is that of an inclusive consciousness: the organization
it achieves as a work of art is . . . an organization that may,
by analogy, be called musical. It exhibits no progression.'[18]

These critics, in the passages I have quoted, looked at the
poem and described it accurately in general terms. But an
adequate critical procedure was lacking. As more and more
information about the *material* of the poem has been made
available, these early critical observations have been set aside.
The raw material has been re-used by critics to construct a
formula, a 'statement of beliefs', which is then said to be *in* the
poem itself. That Eliot went to the trouble of transmuting this
material into non-discursive form is ignored. Mr George Williamson in his 'poem by poem analysis'[19] specifically disagrees with
Leavis's description (quoted above) and proceeds to unfold
what he calls 'the basic scheme' of the poem—a task which he
finds himself able to accomplish *almost entirely without quotation.*
Cleanth Brooks declares of 'The Waste Land':

'The moral of all the incidents which we have been witnessing
is that there must be an asceticism—something to check the
drive of desire.'[20]

—a statement which, again, fails to bring us closer to the poetry.
    I shall discuss a short passage from 'The Waste Land', to-
gether with some of the critical commentaries which deal with it,
in order to distinguish more exactly between what I am declaring
valid and invalid procedures.
    In 'The Fire Sermon' Tiresias observes, and experiences, the
seduction of the typist by the house agent's clerk. Alone after
the event, the 'lovely woman' who has 'stooped to folly'

         'smoothes her hair with automatic hand,
    And puts a record on the gramophone.'

Then follows one of the most beautiful lyric passages in the poem:

> ' "This music crept by me upon the waters"
> And along the Strand, up Queen Victoria Street.
> O City city, I can sometimes hear
> Beside a public bar in Lower Thames Street,
> The pleasant whining of a mandoline
> And a clatter and a chatter from within
> Where fishmen lounge at noon: where the walls
> Of Magnus Martyr hold
> Inexplicable splendour of Ionian white and gold.'

Three commentaries on these lines will illustrate certain points I have been attempting to make about the deficiencies of most criticism of the poem.

Cleanth Brooks[21] considers that the music which 'crept by' the protagonist 'upon the waters' is probably 'O O O O that Shakespeherian Rag', but notes that the latter can also hear, sometimes, the music of the fishmen. This other music—and the location of the fishmen near a church—is 'significant', because the fish is a 'life-symbol'. On the basis of these observations Brooks draws out the statement he believes implicit in the lines:

> 'Life on Lower Thames Street, if not on the Strand, still has meaning as it cannot have meaning for either the typist or the rich woman of "A Game of Chess".'

D. E. S. Maxwell[22] follows Brooks's observations:

> 'The music leads the poem's action to one of the few manifestations of virility in the waste land, in Lower Thames Street, abode of the fishmen, those who continue to give allegiance to the source of life. They live by the river, and by the church.'

George Williamson[23] is at once more abstract and more confident:

> 'The music which creeps by Ferdinand upon the waters of Leman develops the lust or death theme, reveals its moral

significance, and suggests its moral need. Since his fate has been connected with water, water has assumed a fateful attraction for the protagonist, who both fears and craves it. In terms of the fortune the course of these waters is highly significant.'

Later Williamson repeats Brooks's main point.

It will be noticed that these critics are looking for details which are 'significant'—and that 'significance' for each of them resides in the ease with which the chosen details can be accommodated in an abstract system of ideas. But if we return to the lines themselves I think it will be found that none of the remarks quoted above has brought us nearer to their essential quality:

> ' "This music crept by me upon the waters"
> And along the Strand, up Queen Victoria Street.
> O City city, I can sometimes hear
> Beside a public bar in Lower Thames Street,
> The pleasant whining of a mandoline
> And a clatter and a chatter from within
> Where fishmen lounge at noon: where the walls
> Of Magnus Martyr hold
> Inexplicable splendour of Ionian white and gold.'

This passage projects, creates an image of, a particular state of mind. This image or projection is composed out of the indissoluble union of, on the one hand, a particular poetic music, and on the other an edited recreation of the experience—auditory and visual—of a specific time and place. The state is one of melancholy and loneliness in a city, the mind aware of itself alone, quiet and passive, yet on the fringes of human society, noise and action. It is a state of tranquil self-pity and tranquil pleasure. The consciousness of the poem focusses first on the music, which passes it by 'upon the waters'; then on the noises of the pub which it leaves behind; and comes to rest finally on the 'inexplicable splendour' of the silent, solid, visible object.

This is the effect of the lines as they exist alone. Their place in the poem, however, must condition our reading.

Lines 215–56, which precede the passage under discussion, enact a sordid event, in verse whose heroic flavour is capable of both mocking and intensifying the sordidness:

> 'Out of the window perilously spread
> Her drying combinations, touched by the sun's
> last rays . . .'

But the quality achieved in these lines is not precisely that of satire. There is objectivity, 'impersonality' of the kind discussed in Chapter 6; but not the detachment of the satirist who stands apart from the events he describes. There is, perhaps, disgust. But there is also in the lines a caressing quality which lingers upon the events, like Prufrock's smoke over the pools that stand in drains. Tiresias, the poem's 'inclusive consciousness', is sensitive to human degradation. But there is no hint of an implicit moral imperative—no suggestion that such things ought not to happen. This is, in fact, what *happens*, and what must go on happening: it is an image of human life consistent with the state of feeling which governs the poem. The passage is not a detached account of an event, but an *enactment*. The poet's mind is the mind of Tiresias, the 'inclusive consciousness' that has 'fore-suffered all'. But its intimate participation in the event, that mind is released of a common burden; and in this process of enactment and release, Eliot's unique music achieves perfect ease of movement. At the climax of the event, the consciousness of the poem is forced into an indissoluble union with the participants:

> 'And I, Tiresias, have foresuffered all
> Enacted on this same divan or bed;
> I who have sat by Thebes below the wall
> And walked among the lowest of the dead.'

There is in this moment the physical climax of the 'lovers', and the literary climax which forces 'Tiresias' into a humble understanding of himself and of all human kind. What follows can only be peace and sadness, in which the 'lovers', Tiresias, the poet, and his readers (*Vous, hypocrite lecteur!*) concur as one mind.

> 'Well, now that's done: and I'm glad it's over.'

However sordid and mechanical the event has been, the typist's 'half-formed thought' proceeds out of a feeling which is not despair. This is her post-coital sadness, the 'music' of which comes inevitably to the protagonist and creates the equivalent melancholy of the nine lines under specific discussion. So, in these lines, the mind ranges about among impressions, but comes to rest at last on the walls of St Magnus Martyr. The 'inexplicable splendour' is not wholly separated from, nor even a judgement on, the action through which the poem has passed. It is a conclusion generated in the enactment.

In these remarks I have attempted to write some commentary on a direct experience of a passage of the poem. This whole section of 'The Fire Sermon' is, I should think, poetry of the kind described by Eliot in his remarks about 'the first voice' of poetry: it has broken forth from the depths of the mind, after what seems a long gestation, taking its form first as a particular rhythm, gradually solidifying into words, taking into itself a series of visual impressions which in turn attain narrative and symbolic semblance. It is a product of the 'unified sensibility', the imagination heightened, the will kept down to its humble task of arrangement. A critic who is to write adequately of such a passage of poetry cannot, therefore, approach it as if it contained an 'intellectual scheme', slightly obscured, but deliberately planted to be found. If the apparatus of criticism, the notes and the sources, were necessary before the poem could be fully experienced, then 'The Waste Land' would have to be dismissed as inferior poetry. But Eliot clearly meant what he said when he wrote: 'I myself should like an audience which could neither read nor write',[24] and when he argued that poetry could communicate even *before* it was understood. In this he was acknowledging that the experience of his poetry is foremost an aural, emotional experience, one which approximates in many ways to the experience of listening to music; and that an 'intellectual' apparatus can easily impede a full and unified experience of the poetry. One would not, of course, deny all validity to a discussion which draws attention to the anthropological and literary symbolism that has found its way into 'The Waste Land'. But there is clearly a danger that such discussions will offer us Jessie Weston and an assortment of Elizabethan dramatists as a substitute for the poem which ought to be the object of our attention.

'The Hollow Men', Eliot's next completed poem after 'The Waste Land', is interesting because one can trace a number of different attempts to combine its sections into a unit which would form a single poem. Some of the lines seem to belong to sections cancelled by Ezra Pound from 'The Waste Land'; others were written after the publication of 'The Waste Land'. Seven separate sections are used in these different attempts to construct a single poem; five are finally placed in 'The Hollow Men', and the remaining two relegated to the section 'Minor Poems' in the volume *Collected Poems, 1909–35*.

The course of the poem's development may be charted as follows[a]:

Title	First line	Order of writing	Locus
'Song to the Opherian'	The golden foot I may not kiss or clutch. (Contains 'The wind sprang up at four o'clock')	1	*Tyro*, 1922
'Doris's Dream Songs' I	Eyes that last I saw in tears	2	
II	The wind sprang up at four o'clock	1	*Chapbook*, 39, 1924
III	This is the dead land	3	
'Three Poems' I	Eyes I dare not meet in dreams	4	*The Criterion*, III, 10 Jan. 1925
II	Eyes that last I saw in tears	2	
III	The Eyes are not here	5	

[a] D. E. S. Maxwell's incomplete outline of the poem's development, set out as an appendix to his book *The Poetry of T. S. Eliot*, makes one serious error. It prints the twenty-line 'Eyes I dare not meet in dreams' ('The Hollow Men' II) as the first of 'Doris's Dream Songs' from *The Chapbook*, 1924. In fact this section first appeared in *The Criterion*, 1925. The first of 'Doris's Dream Songs' was the fifteen-line 'Eyes that last I saw in tears', now on p. 143 of the *Collected Poems, 1909–35*. This error has not been corrected in the recent paper-back reissue of Maxwell's book.

'The Hollow Men'	I	We are the hollow men	6	*The Dial,* March 1925
	II	Eyes I dare not meet in dreams	4	
	III	The eyes are not here	5	
'The Hollow Men'	I	We are the hollow men	6	*Collected Poems,* pp. 87–90
	II	Eyes I dare not meet in dreams	4	
	III	This is the dead land	3	
	IV	The eyes are not here	5	
	V	Here we go round the prickly pear	7	
'Minor Poems'	I	Eyes that last I saw in tears	2	*Collected Poems,* pp. 143–4
	II	The wind sprang up at four o'clock	1	

For the purpose of this argument the detail to be noted in this procedure is that there is only one major change *within* the separate sections;[a] but the order of the sections is changed over

a This is the change of 'Song to the Opherian' to 'The Wind sprang up at four o'clock'. The latter version is printed on p. 144 of *Collected Poems, 1909–35*. The former has never been reprinted anywhere, and is perhaps worth quoting here. It appeared in *Tyro*, 1922, over the pseudonym 'Gus Krutzch':

'The golden foot I may not kiss or clutch
Glowed in the shadow of the bed
Perhaps it does not come to very much
This thought this ghost this pendulum in the head
Swinging from life to death
Bleeding between two lives
    Waiting that touch.

'The wind sprang up and broke the bells
Is it a dream or something else
When the surface of the blackened river
Is a face that sweats with tears?
I saw across the alien river
The campfire shake the spears.'

and over again. The point is that Eliot seems to regard the separate sections as inviolable—completed poetic entities. His problem is to make them look as though they belong together, as he feels they must since they have sprung from a common node of feeling. But he must join them into a single structure without damaging any one of them internally. The structure, then, is a secondary matter, a problem considered only after the writing is complete. It is a matter of conscious arrangement. And the difficulty of achieving a semblance of structure is indicated by the variety of orders attempted:

I				
2,	I,	3		
4,	2,	5		
6,	4,	5		
6,	4,	3,	5,	7
2,	I			

If we keep this procedure in mind, and remember too that when Pound excised almost one third of the original 'Waste Land' Eliot felt the poem had been *improved*, it will be seen to what extent the structural unity of his early poetry is a unity of feeling, and how inappropriate any analysis is which treats it as an intellectual scheme. It will be seen, too, that we are dealing with poetry different in kind from most other poetry in English: few poems would survive cutting of the kind applied to 'The Waste Land', or the shuffling imposed on 'The Hollow Men'.

'Ash Wednesday' is another poem constructed from a number of separate moments of what might be called 'creative emotion'. Its imagery draws on areas of experience different from those which provide the imagery of 'The Waste Land'; but as poetry it is not different in kind. It is not until *Four Quartets* that we find what seems an important change in Eliot's methods of composition; and the change is exhibited principally in a considerable increase in structural ordering, both of the poem as a whole and of its parts. Our principal observation about *Four Quartets* can be put at its simplest, then, if we say that the poem would be seriously damaged by any large-scale cutting or reshuffling of the kind applied to Eliot's earlier poetry. It is a poem constructed piece by piece into a pattern, the coherence of which contributes to what it has to communicate. The poem has been directed, however gently, by the conscious will. It exhibits progression of a kind lacking in all of Eliot's earlier (non-dramatic) poetry. There is still very little in it that is argued or rhetorically affirmed. But one would never find in his earlier work such lecture-room pronouncements as

> 'There is, it seems to us,
> At best, only a limited value
> In the knowledge derived from experience.'

Four Quartets is a series of variations on themes which are 'traditional', 'orthodox', in a sense unarguable. Thus 'inspiration' is possible, but only *within* the framework which is fixed as it is not in 'The Waste Land'. 'Texture' can only flow into a structure whose inception has preceded it.

Since it is this structure that distinguishes the poem from Eliot's other poetry (and there is, so far as I know, no discussion of *Four Quartets* which sets the structure out with any exactness), it will be as well to sketch it in outline before proceeding to discuss the poetry.

In each Quartet the five sections follow patterns which are sufficiently alike for the following general descriptions to apply in each case.

I   The movement of time, in which brief moments of eternity are caught.
II Worldly experience, leading only to dissatisfaction.
III Purgation in the world—divesting the soul of the love of created things—expressed mainly in terms of present movement, a journey which is freedom from past and future.
IV A lyric prayer for, or affirmation of the need of, Intercession.
V   The problems of attaining artistic wholeness which become analogues for, and merge in to, the problems of achieving spiritual health.

I shall try to make clearer this basic similarity of each group of parallel sections; but it should be noted that to set the pattern out as I have done below is to suggest a more rigorous mould than the poem in fact displays. My intention is only to indicate that the pattern is there, not to press my descriptions too far.

Section I of each Quartet:

The attainment, in time, of brief moments of eternity.

(1) 'Burnt Norton' I (basic element—air)

The passage leading to an open door (time).

The garden (innocence) briefly transformed in time.

| Out of the air the voices of innocence | ⎧ 'echoes'
⎨ 'the lotus'
⎩ the laughter
    of children | ⎫ These are images of
⎬ the permanence of
⎭ innocence in time. |

(2) 'East Coker' I (basic element—earth)

Houses, roads, factories—rising and falling, changing (time).

The field (fertility) briefly transformed in time.

| Out of the earth the music of propagation | ⎧ the dancing
⎨ figures—
⎪ 'signifying
⎩ matrimonie' | ⎫ These are images
⎪ of the permanence
⎬ of 'experience', of
⎭ the flesh, in time. |

(3) 'The Dry Salvages' I (basic element—water)

The river and the sea as erosive forces (time)

The sea (as an image of original chaos) throws up evidence of death.

| Out of the sea the voices of death | ⎧ sea howl, yelp, rote of
⎨ granite teeth, groaner,
⎩ bell | ⎫ These are images of
⎬ the permanence of
⎭ death in time. |

(4) 'Little Gidding' I (basic element—fire)

The changes of the seasons (time).

Midwinter ice briefly transformed to fire in the seasonal paradoxes.

| Out of the fires the voices of eternity | ⎧ 'the communication of
⎨ the dead is tongued
⎩ with fire' | ⎫ This is an image of
⎬ the permanence of
⎭ eternity in time. |

Section II of each Quartet:

The world offers no enduring satisfaction; in these sections all attempt to escape from it seems vain.

(1) 'Burnt Norton' II

Formal lyric: an attempt to establish links which ought to exist between the worlds of flesh and spirit.

Discursive passage which looks towards a point at which the tensions of the world are resolved. The lines circle about this point as a concept, but fail to achieve it.

(2) 'East Coker' II

Formal lyric: an attempt to link the events of the earthly seasons with the more spectacular revolutions of the heavens.

Discursive passage on the subject of old age. Age offers no special knowledge, no solution to the problems of living. The only wisdom is humility.

(3) 'The Dry Salvages' II

Formal lyric: telling over the endless destructive force of time, specifically in terms of sailing and the sea.

Discursive passage on the subject of time seen in old age as the destroyer of moments of illumination and the preserver of remembered agony.

(4) 'Little Gidding' II

Formal lyric: the destruction of the physical world by a resolution to its basic elements—air, earth, fire, and water.

Discursive passage (though much less casual, more carefully and finely wrought than any of its equivalent passages) in which the 'dead master' outlines the empty honours offered by the world to its aging great men.

Section III of each Quartet:

Escape from the world is discovered in the present—in a freeing of the self from past and future, from memory and desire. Concentration on the journey which is the present offers the only area in which the world may be transcended.

(1) 'Burnt Norton' III

Experience of travelling in the London underground, used as an image of the purgation of worldly love. This is achieved by a concentration in the present which looks neither forward nor back.

> 'Here is a place of disaffection
> Time before and time after
> In a dim light.'

(2) 'East Coker' III

The great men of the world travel into the darkness of the future, aware of the darkness of the past recorded in almanacs and directories. Again this section affirms a concentration in the present, vacating the mind of its worldly desires—as in

> 'the darkened theatre
> the tube train stopped between stations
> the mind under ether.'

This process is then seen in a different way as a journey of the mind between opposing sets of abstractions (last 12 lines).

(3) 'The Dry Salvages' III

The images of a journey are explicit here. The travellers should 'fare foreward', conscious of neither the point of departure nor the destination:

> 'Here between the hither and the farther shore
> While time is withdrawn.'

(4) 'Little Gidding' III

Looks to the achievement of a correct 'indifference', which grows between 'attachment' and 'detachment'—

> '. . . and so liberation
> From future as well as past.'

This liberation through 'indifference' should also occur in the journey which is history.

Section IV of each Quartet:
The lyric prayer for, or affirmation of the need of, Intercession.

(1) 'Burt Norton' IV

A lyric questioning the possibility of Intercession in the natural world.

(2) 'East Coker' IV

Formal lyric affirming the Intercession of Christ as 'the wounded surgeon', operating in his 'hospital', the world, which was 'endowed' by 'the ruined millionaire' Adam.

(3) 'The Dry Salvages' IV

Lyric prayer to the Virgin for Intercession.

(4) 'Little Gidding' IV

Formal lyric affirming the Intercession of God as Love.

Section V of each Quartet:

The specific problems of achieving good art merge, in each case, into the problems of achieving the good life. Goodness, health, in both the particular ('art') and the general ('life') depend largely upon various kinds of precision.

In each of these fifth sections the artistic effort serves as an analogue for the spiritual effort.

(1) 'Burnt Norton' V

The work of art as movement in which stillness is attained.

The difficulties of precision in art ('Words strain/Crack, and sometimes break . . .')

The problems of art merge into the problems of life: the attainment of a 'still centre' is the object in both.

(2) 'East Coker' V

The practice of an art seen as a continual exploration of the means of communication.

The difficulties of precision in art ('With shabby equipment always deteriorating . . .')

The problems of art merge into the problems of life—life is a continual exploration of the means of communication ('communion') with God. In both the desire is to achieve greater intensity.

(3) 'The Dry Salvages' V

The false arts, which draw on false traditions, are inevitable
wrong attempts to apprehend 'the point of intersection of the
timeless/With time . . .'
But precision in such experience is attained only by the discipline
of the Saint, not by false agents.
The object of these false arts—a momentary release from time—
is achieved in life (if at all) only by 'hints and guesses'.

(4) 'Little Gidding' V

The work of art seen as a perfect unity, a poem capable both of
development in time and the attainment of timeless moments.
Precision is again emphasized ('And every phrase/And sentence
that is right . . .')
The achievement of art merges into the achievement of life—the
discovery of a *form* in life capable, like the forms of art, both
of development in time and of timeless moments.

These descriptions of each group of parallel sections emphasize
common themes. But within the general theme set for each section
there is considerable freedom, and hence a considerable range of
thought and feeling. Nevertheless the change from Eliot's earlier
methods of composition is a radical one. The plan must have
been drafted before the writing began, or at least was fixed by the
time 'Burnt Norton' was finished. 'Inspiration', the unwilled
creative moment, is still possible within the general framework,
but only if it can be used to further one or another relevant
theme.

Four Quartets is an attempt to bring into a more exact balance
the will and the creative imagination; it attempts to harness the
creative imagination which in all Eliot's earlier poetry ran its
own course, edited but not consciously directed. The achievement is of a high order, but the best qualities of *Four Quartets*
are inevitably different from those of 'The Waste Land'.

The place of 'The Waste Land' in the piece of literary history
which is the concern of this book has already been defined. The
poem is the final realization of an impulse directed against
poetic discourse. It is a poem which refuses to be anything else
but poetry. This is not to say that it fulfils simple doctrines of

'Art for Art's Sake', but that it is in no sense an agent or instrument of the will. Its virtue resides in its completeness as an entity uniting 'aesthetic' and 'moral' qualities into a fusion which, transcending both, acquires life. The poem *is*; it has a being. Or, to put the matter differently, it has a quality which calls forth organic metaphors when we attempt to describe it. It achieves 'impersonality' of a kind which *Four Quartets*, with its many discursive passages and its consciously controlled plan, does not attempt.

The English poetic tradition has always occupied middleground between pure discourse and pure Image. At times it has striven hard towards the Image; at others it has been content to be scarcely distinguished from prose except by its metrical form. At any point where it became *pure* discourse it ceased to be poetry. On the other hand the number of occasions on which it has become pure Image are so few that no generalization can safely be made about them. Two points at which this purity has been significantly achieved are 'The Waste Land' and 'Ash Wednesday'. But Eliot's development since 1935 suggests that the achievement left him dissatisfied, or left him feeling that he was, as a poet, 'helpless before the contents of his own mind'[25] —a feeling he was not willing to tolerate. In these two poems Eliot achieves his mature style, but it is a style dependent to a large extent on moments he can only in a general way predict or control. In *Four Quartets* he sets out to undo that style, and to achieve another—one in which there would be more of his conscious self, his personality, his wisdom. Yeats's explanation of the change observed in his style after 1909 is not altogether irrevelant here: 'I have tried to make my work convincing, with a speech so natural and dramatic that the hearer would feel the presence of a man thinking and feeling.'[26] There are values the poet wants, not simply incorporated into the texture of his lines, but *affirmed*. By means of his theory of the dramatic mask, Yeats found his way from the passive music of his early poems to the affirming energy of his later work, without any serious intrusion of 'personality'. In *Four Quartets* there is, I think, the same impulse to take up a more usual middle-ground position between the extremes of discourse and the Image. 'Wisdom', an ordered construction upon 'felt life', enters Eliot's later poetry as it enters Yeats's. The question which remains to be answered—or at least put—is whether the style of *Four Quartets* carries the burden satisfactorily. In the view of this argument it does not.

In his early poetry Eliot perfected the non-discursive medium —as Yeats failed to perfect it in the 1890's—to such a degree that he turns to his new task with no ready method for making poetry of the personal voice:

> 'So here I am, in the middle way, having had
> twenty years—
> Twenty years largely wasted, the years of
> *l'entre deux guerres*—
> Trying to learn to use words, and every attempt
> Is a wholly new start, and a different kind of
> failure
> Because one has only learned to get the better of
> words
> For the thing one no longer has to say, or the way
> in which
> One is no longer disposed to say it.'
>
> 'East Coker' V

There is truth in this, but not imaginative truth: it remains *pure* discourse. If the feeling of failure is truly there, it is there unused; it has not been transmuted by imagination into something larger than itself.

Four Quartets alternates between, on the one hand the 'first voice' of poetry, the voice of 'The Waste Land', less perfect now because directed into a conscious mould; and on the other the 'second voice', the voice of the man 'addressing an audience' in verse barely distinguished from prose. The poem is the expression of a personality so fine, so mature, and so supremely intelligent, that to question the achievement may seem only to quibble. But however wise and admirable the man it displays, the poem remains, in this view, imperfectly achieved, with large portions of abstraction untransmuted into the living matter of poetry. This, then, is the point of a remark made at the opening of this chapter: that it is the very success of a method, achieved in 'The Waste Land', that keeps Eliot short of greatness in the other.

The discourse of *Four Quartets* points constantly towards 'the unattended moment'—

> . . . 'the moment in and out of time,
> The distraction fit, lost in a shaft of sunlight. . . .'
>
> 'The Dry Salvages' V

In these timeless moments, communion with the Infinite has been achieved; but they lie *outside* the poem and can only be indicated, not entered, and hardly described:

> 'I can only say *there* we have been, but I
> cannot say where.'
>
> 'Burnt Norton' II

These are assurances that Eliot the man has achieved such moments; there is no longer a 'sensuous re-creation' of the moment itself. Formerly these timeless moments were the moments of literary creation. Now they are private moments between the man and the Infinite, and only discourse can assure us of their occurrence. The poet's concentration is now beyond the world. He has (in the words of St John of the Cross quoted as epigraph to 'Sweeney Agonistes') attempted to divest his soul of the love of created things in order that it may be possessed of the Divine Union. But it is *in* the world, *in* the love of created things, that poetry is generated and takes life. So one is left feeling, after many passages of the poem, that Eliot is saying in a more elaborate way what Orestes says in the other epigraph to the Sweeney poems:

> 'You don't see them, you don't—but I see them:
> they are hunting me down. I must move on.'

We believe in the poet's experience. The voice is intense and convincing, but too often intensely personal, the voice of one man, not of humanity. And when an attempt is made to broaden the significance of this personal experience, the poem comes to grief among abstractions:

> 'You say I am repeating
> Something I have said before. I shall say it again.
> Shall I say it again? In order to arrive there,

> To arrive where you are, to get from where you are not,
>   You must go by a way wherein there is no ecstasy.
> In order to arrive at what you do not know
>   You must go by a way which is the way of ignorance.
> In order to possess what you do not possess
>   You must go by the way of dispossession.
> In order to arrive at what you are not
>   You must go through the way in which you are not.
> And what you do not know is the only thing you know
> And what you own is what you do not own
> And where you are is where you are not.'
>
>   'East Coker' III

What this means is the only thing it means; and what it strives to be is what it is not.

It is not surprising then that the finest passages in *Four Quartets* (that there *are* fine passages needs, of course, no special acknowledgement) are passages which run counter to the planned intention of the poem. The lines take life when they are permitted to rest for a moment in the physical world, permitted to express 'the love of created things':

>   'Now the light falls
> Across the open field, leaving the lane
> Shuttered with branches, dark in the afternoon,
> Where you lean against a bank while a van passes,
> And the deep lane insists on the direction
> Into the village, in the electric heat
> Hypnotised. In a warm haze the sultry light
> Is absorbed, not refracted, by grey stone.
> The dahlias sleep in the empty silence.
> Wait for the early owl.'
>
>   'East Coker' I

Here the poet's feeling takes form in experiencing the visible world, where it is content to rest; only the imposed plan, not the feeling, insists that such experience is unsatisfying, and presses towards abstraction.

In 'East Coker' III the deliberate renunciation of the world is again described:

'I said to my soul be still, and wait without hope
For hope would be hope for the wrong thing; wait without love
For love would be love for the wrong thing; there is yet faith
But the faith and the love and the hope are all in the waiting.
Wait without thought for you are not ready for thought:
So the darkness shall be light, and the stillness the dancing.'

This is a description of the vacation of the conscious mind as a preparation for inspiration—in this case divine inspiration. It is a state of mind clearly related to that in which the poet waits for literary inspiration—the state Eliot described twenty years earlier, in a context which confined it to the writing of poetry, as 'a passive attending upon the event'.[27] Now we are offered only a direction *towards* the experience, not the experience itself. Yet against the will of the man the habit of the poet constantly struggles towards concretion. Despite the conscious plan, the poetry appears and reappears, impatient to assume the world:

'Dawn points, and another day
Prepares for heat and silence. Out at sea the dawn wind
Wrinkles and slides.'

Lines like these do not advance the plan at all: they represent a moment of poetry, a brief, exact crystallization of feeling, which Eliot could not forgo.

It has been argued in this chapter and the last that one of the commonest mistakes of contemporary criticism has been to describe Eliot as an 'intellectual' poet, meaning by this a poet entirely conscious and deliberate in writing his poetry. In *Four Quartets* there are many attempts to write in a style which, if the attempts had succeeded, would have justified the description; but in these passages expressing conscious ideas and beliefs poetry is rarely achieved. Some of the more obvious examples, where Eliot speaks in the manner of the public lecturer, have already been quoted. These are only with difficulty described as poetry. On the other hand they are not, I think, the least successful passages in the poem:

'I have said before
That the experience revived in the meaning
Is not the experience of one life only

But of many generations—not forgetting
Something that is probably quite ineffable:
The backward look behind the assurance
Of recorded history, the backward half-look
Over the shoulder towards the primitive terror.'

'The Dry Salvages' II

This is, or is very nearly, pure prose discourse. Yet it remains an honest 'second voice', the voice of the public man whose personality we can recognize, whose intellect we admire, and whose ideas we have learned to approach at least with the caution of a bomb-disposal unit. 'I have said before' calls the class to attention, and we accept the lecture with only a little shuffling in the back rows. There is, however, another operation of the 'meddling intellect' for which neither his poetic practice nor his experience as a lecturer have prepared Eliot: the conscious working up into verse, through a series of intellectual analogies and paradoxes, of a 'metaphysical' idea. Section IV of 'East Coker' is an example of this; and the result is one of the few sections which not merely fail to be good poetry, but succeed in being thoroughly bad. The lines exploit and enlarge upon a number of traditional 'paradoxes': we must die in order to live; our 'disease' is our hope of 'health' (the paradox of the Fortunate Fall); the flesh and blood of Christ are the means of the spirit's escape from flesh and blood.

'The wounded surgeon plies the steel
 That questions the distempered part;
 Beneath the bleeding hands we feel
 The sharp compassion of the healer's art
 Resolving the enigma of the fever chart.

'Our only health is the disease
 If we obey the dying nurse
 Whose constant care is not to please
 But to remind of our, and Adam's curse,
 And that, to be restored, our sickness must grow worse.'

Eliot works these paradoxes out, through a demanding verse form, with the rigorous exactness of a compiler of crossword puzzles. The result is a piece of ingenuity, a synthetic poem, quite without feeling or life. Many of Donne's poems exploit analogies and paradoxes of this kind. The difference is that for Donne the 'ideas' are there, not for their own sake, but only to serve the emotion which generates the poem and takes substance in it. If one analogy ceases to be useful, it is dropped and another taken up; Donne's 'logic' is more apparent than real. His intellect, as Eliot has said, is at the tips of his senses; and it is there only in order that the demands of feeling may be served. In 'The Wounded surgeon . . .' Eliot expresses only an abstract idea. He has, in short, attempted a style alien to his own development, and remote from the truest impulses of his poetic sensibility.[a]

On the other hand, achievement must be acknowledged. Throughout *Four Quartets* the uneasy alliance of discourse and Image gains strength. 'Little Gidding' comes closest of the four Quartets to achieving completeness and unity. In its opening twenty lines particularly, the divided impulses of the poem come together. Attention is focussed on the physical world; yet the visible scene carries an abstract idea, entirely incorporated into the rich texture of the lines, so that the scene itself is transmuted, the physical world acquiring a strange *meta*physical intensity:

> 'When the short day is brightest, with frost and fire,
> The brief sun flames the ice, on pond and ditches,
> In windless cold that is the heart's heat,
> Reflecting in a watery mirror
> A glow that is blindness in the early afternoon.
> And glow more intense than blaze of branch, or brazier,
> Stirs the dumb spirit: no wind, but pentecostal fire
> In the dark time of year. Between melting and freezing
> The soul's sap quivers. There is no earth smell
> Or smell of living thing.'

Paradoxes the poem has already exploited in a number of ways can be found again in these lines. Midwinter is the soul's spring,

a We may perhaps indicate the failure of this poem in another way if we recall Eliot's definition of metaphysical wit, which includes the remark 'It involves, probably, a recognition, implicit in the expression of every experience, of other kinds of experience which are possible'. 'Andrew Marvell', *Selected Essays*, p. 303.

for it anticipates the 'unimaginable/Zero summer' after death. Its 'windless cold . . . is the heart's heat' which looks beyond 'the scheme of generation'. Yet here the abstractions come to life, because they assume their form in the physical world, in 'the love of created things'.

'Style,' as the Introduction to this book describes it, is the poet's way of knowing his world; it is a way of re-creating a world of experience. A failure of style, whether the work is simple description or something more complex, is a false report, the creation of an image which misrepresents 'things as they are'. Hence the conclusion reached in Chapter 6, that Eliot's conception of style, correctly read where it is best expressed, transcends 'aesthetics' as a concern with beauty, and 'morals' as a set of truths which imply imperatives for right action, fusing the two in a poetics from which neither is detachable. It follows that in such a view, a literary heresy is also inevitably and concomitantly a heresy in a wider sense. The poet, for example, who denies the world in favour of his own abstract thought is in danger of becoming a 'personality', imposing *himself* on the world instead of acting as a medium between it and his readers; he is claiming too much for his own point of the 'triangle'. Likewise, in the wider sense of heresy, the man who denies the world in order to perfect his soul may be in danger of the sin of pride. In the more abstract sections of *Four Quartets* both heresies occur, and the two are one:

> 'Only a flicker
> Over the strained time-ridden faces
> Distracted from distraction by distraction
> Filled with fancies and empty of meaning
> Tumid apathy with no concentration
> Men and bits of paper, whirled by the cold wind
> That blows before and after time,
> Wind in and out of unwholesome lungs
> Time before and time after
> Eructation of unhealthy souls
> Into the faded air . . .'[a]

[a] 'Burnt Norton' III. A literary antecedent of the attitude here presented may be found in Aldington's poem 'A Row of Eyes . . .', quoted in Chapter 5, p. 106.

Here is a piece of 'fine writing'; but it is also a view of the world which is 'personal' or 'subjective' in a dangerous sense. It is, insofar as it claims the authority of generalization, a false report, for it sells the world short in order that the world may be unlovable. One must love created things in order that one may have love to divest. And one enters the world of imagination—or spirit—only by contemplating with love, not by renouncing, the immediate and the particular. The 'unified sensibility' is in itself a kind of 'divine union', and the will-driven intellect may not achieve it alone.

These remarks, if they are meaningful, indicate the shortcomings of much of the poem, and also the particular success of the opening of 'Little Gidding'. In those twenty lines we have almost the only point in the poem at which a perfect balance is achieved between the rightful claims of flesh and spirit.

The literary scene upon which Eliot came as a young man has been sketched in Chapters 3 to 5. He, like Yeats, found judgement according to 'meaning' predominating over more adequate methods of criticism; and he, again like Yeats, took temporary refuge in his own kind of 'aestheticism'. But Eliot not only affirmed the Symbolists' non-discursive mode; he perfected it.

The accumulated discontent of Pre-Raphaelites, Aesthetes, Georgians, and Imagists, together with social upheaval during and following the war, combined to establish gradually a context in which new attitudes to the study and criticism of poetry were accepted. Now it was possible to relax the aesthete's posture, both in its attitude to an audience, and in its absolute insistence on an 'impersonal' relationship between the poet and his world of experience. Eliot, an Anglican, wished not merely to make, but to *affirm*. In 'The Waste Land' he had brought his world of experience to life. In *Four Quartets* he attempts both to re-make and to pass judgement upon that world; but in the view this book has taken, he does not succeed completely in the later plan. 'The Waste Land' remains, historically at least, his great achievement.

REFERENCES

1. *A Reader's Guide to T. S. Eliot*, p. 63.
2. ibid., p. 16.
3. *A Vision*, 1937 edition, p. 4.
4. Cleanth Brooks, *Modern Poetry and the Tradition*, p. 170.
5. *An Approach to Hamlet*, 1960, p. 74.
6. *The Invisible Poet*, p. 35.
7. *Letters of Ezra Pound*, p. 92.
8. *The Symbolist Movement in Literature*, Arthur Symons, p. 108.
9. See Chapter 5, p. 97.
10. *Oxford Book of Modern Verse*, 1936. Introduction, p. xxii.
11. *Bishop Berkeley*, Hone and Rossi, with an introduction by W. B. Yeats, 1931. Introduction, p. xxiv.
12. See Chapter 6.
13. *The Invisible Poet*, pp. 125 and ff.
14. 'The Metaphysical Poets', *Selected Essays*, p. 287.
15. 'Tradition and the Individual Talent', ibid.
16. *The Achievement of T. S. Eliot*, p. 15. Italics mine.
17. *The Hound and the Horn*, vol. I, no. 3, 1928, p. 195. Italics mine.
18. *New Bearings in English Poetry*, p. 103.
19. *A Reader's Guide to T. S. Eliot*, pp. 121 and 126.
20. *Modern Poetry and the Tradition*, p. 156.
21. ibid., p. 154.
22. *The Poetry of T. S. Eliot*, 1952, p. 110.
23. *A Reader's Guide . . .* , p. 128.
24. *The Use of Poetry . . .* , p. 152.
25. W. B. Yeats, see p. 157 above.
26. *Letters of W. B. Yeats*, p. 583. Quoted Chapter 2.
27. 'Tradition and the Individual Talent'. *Selected Essays*, p. 21.

8

CONCLUSION

'O chestnut-tree, great-rooted blossomer,
Are you the leaf, the blossom or the bole?
O body swayed to music, O brightening glance,
How can we know the dancer from the dance?'
                    W. B. YEATS: 'Among School Children'

IN ORDER to indicate the area of study with which this book
was to concern itself, a metaphor was offered, in Chapter 1, of a
triangle whose points were the poet, the world of experience
which provides his subject matter, and the audience. Attention
has been concentrated on two lines of tension in this 'triangle'—
one between the poet and his audience, another between the
poet and his 'subject-matter'. It has also been argued that these
two lines of tension constitute one problem for the poet engaged
in writing his poem: an adjustment of one line of a triangle is
also inevitably the adjustment of another. What, for example, in
terms of this metaphor, are the implications of the following
report in 'Books Received', the *Athenaeum*, 6 June 1919?

'John Oxenham *All Clear!* a book of verse commemorative of
the great peace. Methuen 1919.

 '*All Clear!* tells in fervent verse how after the crisis and
calamities of the war "Christ came to earth again". The other
pieces are hymns of praise. "Completing 25,000 copies" is the
legend on the cover—a fact of no literary interest.'

It should be clear why the *Athenaeum*, newly constituted after
the war under the editorship of John Middleton Murry, should
consider rapid sales 'of no literary interest'. *All Clear!* offers,
in metrical form, the thoughts and emotions of a simple man
who has only an elementary knowledge of the powers and the

limitations of the words he uses. It is a book which simplifies almost beyond recognition four years of complex experience. It arrives at conclusions which are easy and acceptable to most literate human beings, not necessarily because

> 'human kind
> Cannot bear very much reality'

> ('Burnt Norton' I)

but because human kind for the most part understands reality better than it understands the processes by which the language is used to embody it. 'Poetry', after all (so the popular argument goes), is not 'Life'. So John Oxenham lengthens the line between himself and 'reality' or 'truth', and succeeds—for as long as commercial interests find it expedient to hold him before the public—in shortening the line between himself and 'poetry-lovers'. His 25,000 buyers will hail him as a poet while they continue to remember, or be reminded of, his name.

Oxenham's book represents the kind of imbalance which the best poets of this century have worked to eliminate. An article, three years earlier in the same periodical, which greeted 'selections from the work of Mr Ezra Pound, Mr Lee Masters, Mr T. S. Eliot, and others' as 'a trick' and 'a pose',[1] or a review of a book of poems by D. H. Lawrence which spoke of 'self-communings, morbid ecstasies, repulsions and ravings'[2]—these articles indicate how tenuous the line between poet and audience became when the poet attempted to look closely into those complexities in experience which poets like Oxenham preferred to ignore.

This book has followed the course of a struggle to adjust the proportions of the 'triangle' in England from 1909 to 1920; and it has attempted to show in what ways this struggle influenced directions taken, at various points in their careers, by Eliot and Yeats. It has traced the gradual success among a few men of an effort to balance the poet's public and private responsibilities. No attempt has been made to cover the whole range of twentieth-century English poetry, but only a period of sufficient scope to illustrate succinctly the nature and consequences of the problem.

In studying the course of this struggle between poets and 'poetry-lovers', several frequently repeated critical estimates have been called into question. If the evidence here assembled is accepted, it is no longer possible, for example, to 'write off' the Georgians with that confidence which has become almost mechanical in recent criticism. We must grant them at least *historical* importance, and must refuse to accept generalizations of the kind with which D. E. S. Maxwell opens the first chapter of his book *The Poetry of T. S. Eliot*:

'From 1900 until the First World War, poetry in England wandered for the most part along country paths opened up by the nineteenth-century romantics, unaware that the paths had become ruts, and that a more suitable track was now the pavement. New forces were appearing, but their influence was small, and on the Georgians, who commanded what popular favour there was, non-existent.'

Maxwell is typical, I think, of most recent critics of twentieth-century poetry. He shows no awareness that there were poets more popular than the Georgians at this time; that the group which this book has called 'Imperialist poets' considered the Georgians dangerous young innovators; that the Georgians were consciously narrowing the scope of poetry in order that certain common literary vices might be excluded; and that their efforts made possible both the war poetry of Wilfred Owen and the mature poetry of Robert Graves. J. C. Squire's Georgians of the early 1920's—the Squirearchy', as Osbert Sitwell called them—must not be confused with the group of liberal intellectuals which congregated around 'Eddie' Marsh in 1911, any more than the original Imagists should be confused with the later 'Amygists' (see chapter 5, pp. 97–8).

This incorrect view of the literary background is related to another incorrect view also exemplified in Maxwell's opening chapter: that which shows Eliot as a new classicist, independent of the problems and impulses which flow out of the Romantic movement. If this study has achieved its purpose, it should have indicated that Eliot as much as Yeats was concerned to bring together two impulses which had separated out of romanticism, and which had gone on widening in their separation throughout the nineteenth century. On the one hand there was, as Chapter 1 suggests, a discursive mode which had come to dominate English poetry in the Victorian age, and which was the mode approved by the reading public. On the other hand there was the non-discursive mode—that which drove the poet towards the irreducible Image. Matthew Arnold is perhaps a good example of a critic caught between the two—on the one hand scolding discursiveness, 'the modern English habit' (as he describes it in a letter) 'too much encouraged by Wordsworth of using poetry as a channel for thinking aloud'; on the other hand arguing that good poetry is 'a criticism of life'. With one foot on 'natural magic' and the other on 'moral interpretation', and with a sense that the two were moving apart, Arnold wrote essays which have made him appear to some the upholder of a flavourless moralist tradition in criticism, and to others the father of aestheticism. This in itself may be a tribute to the balance of his critical mind; and certainly a close reading of his essay on Wordsworth is indispensible to a proper understanding of our critical history. Arnold bequeaths these problems to twentieth-century criticism, and no poet or critic of importance can fail to consider them.[a] They are, ultimately, the problems of Romanticism, and Eliot is no more independent of them than Yeats. We need only remind ourselves of Arnold's judgement of the poetry of Dryden and Pope, and then of Eliot's essay 'The Three Voices of Poetry', to see the continuity of the argument:

'The difference between genuine poetry and the poetry of Dryden, Pope, and all their school [Arnold writes], is briefly this: their poetry is conceived and composed in their wits, genuine poetry is conceived and composed in the soul.'[3]

Arnold is saying what Eliot has, in his own way, said again: that their poetry is not essentially of the 'first voice', of the Image; it proceeds from no 'dark embryo' buried deep in the 'soul', the 'unconscious', the unknowable self. The difference between Arnold and Eliot is that Eliot allows the 'second voice' its rightful place. There is a difference of evaluation, but not of definition. And the definition both men offer is a Romantic—and a respectable—one.

There is, then, a tradition of thought and argument about poetry to which Eliot inevitably belongs; and that tradition,

[a] These sentences are a revision of those I wrote in the first edition of this book where, it now seems to me I did less than justice to Arnold. C. K. S.

whatever it takes over from French writers, runs unbroken from the Romantics.

Despite the powerful resistance of the reading public, it is away from discourse and towards the Image that the most vigorous poetic minds have striven during the years studied in this essay. But they have striven in that direction in order to achieve middle-ground, in order to escape from the popular discursiveness of Victorian poetry. Yeats and Eliot have employed quite different techniques, but in each case the principal effort has been to avoid the isolation of 'aesthetic' and 'moral' qualities in poetry, to achieve a fusion of these into a new wholeness. And this new wholeness could only be achieved by a radical readjustment of the proportions of the 'triangle'. In the writing of their best poetry, each found his own way to set his audience on the one hand, and his experience on the other, at a correct distance.

What, then, is the poet's function which the achievements of Eliot and Yeats, and of many less talented but equally devoted poets of this century, imply? It is not to instruct, nor is it simply to delight; it is not to state Truth only, nor to create Beauty. To say that the function is to delight *and* instruct, to state truth *and* create beauty, will not do either; for such a description implies still that separation of functions against which the whole effort of the best contemporary poetry and criticism has been directed. Neither the terms of morals nor the terms of aesthetics will serve. We can only conclude that there is, unformulated in this effort of the contemporary mind, a new poetic which requires of the poet's sensibility that it should draw into itself both moral and aesthetic qualities latent in the raw materials of the art, fusing these qualities into a form richer, more alive, more intensely expressive of the full human condition, than any other form of which man is capable; a poetic which requires that this should be done despite the forces of discursive mediocrity directed against it—that it should be done despite, and for, the vast new reading public which knows little or nothing of the effort.

REFERENCES

1. *Athenaeum*, February 1916, p. 73.
2. ibid., February 1918, p. 103.
3. 'Thomas Gray', *Essays in Criticism*, Second Series, 1888.

INDEX

The more important references are italicized

193

ACKNOWLEDGEMENTS

I should like to thank the University of Bristol for its award of the Michael Hiatt Baker Scholarship which made possible the research recorded in this book.

My consciousness of a debt to Professor L. C. Knights for his generous and patient help during many discussions of my work finds no ready formula, and can only be acknowledged here gratefully and inadequately.

I am grateful to the following for permission to quote copyright material: the Executors of the Estate of Richard Aldington for extracts from 'Epilogue' and 'In the Tube' in *Complete Poems;* The Bodley Head Ltd for extracts from *Return to Yesterday* by Ford Madox Ford; Chatto & Windus Ltd for extracts from 'Dulce et Decorum Est' and 'The Parable of the Old Men and the Young' in *Poems* by Wilfred Owen; André Deutsch Ltd for extracts from 'The hard sand breaks . . .', 'Thou art come at length . . .' and 'Whirl up, sea . . .' by Hilda Doolittle; Mr T. S. Eliot and Faber & Faber Ltd for extracts from 'La Figlia Che Piange', 'The Love Song of J. Alfred Prufrock' and 'Whispers of Immortality' in *Collected Poems* and extracts from *Four Quartets;* Mr E. M. Forster and Edward Arnold (Publishers) Ltd for an extract from *Howards End;* the Executors of the late W. W. Gibson for 'Geraniums' in *Solway Ford and Other Poems;* Mr Joseph Hone and Macmillan & Co. Ltd for an extract from *W. B. Yeats 1865-1939;* the Estate of the late Mrs Frieda Lawrence and Laurence Pollinger Ltd for an extract from *Phoenix* by D. H. Lawrence; Mr Patrick MacGill and Herbert Jenkins Ltd for an extract from *Songs of the Dead End;* John Murray (Publishers) Ltd for extracts from 'The Best School of All', 'Clifton Chapel', 'Minora Sidera', 'The Vigil' and 'Vitai Lampada' in *Poems:*

New and Old by Sir Henry Newbolt and *The Later Life and Letters* of *Sir Henry Newbolt,* and an extract from *Collected Poems* by Alfred Noyes; the Executors of the Estate of John Oxenham for an extract from 'All's Well!'; Mr Ezra Pound for an extract from 'Mr Nixon' in *Collected Shorter Poems;* Sidgwick & Jackson Ltd for extracts from *Collected Poems of Rubert Brooke;* the Society of Authors for extracts from 'Desolation,' *The Man Who Saw and Other Poems Arising Out of the War* and *The Purple East* by Sir William Watson; Mr Arthur Symons and William Heinemann Ltd for an extract from *The Symbolist Movement in Literature;* Mrs. Helen Thomas for 'July' and 'Tonight' in *Collected Poems of Edward Thomas;* Mrs W. B. Yeats and Macmillan & Co Ltd for extracts from 'Easter 1916' and 'The Fisherman' in *Collected Poems of W. B. Yeats.*

DATE DUE			

WITHDRAWN

GAYLORD FR2